The Oxford Guide to
OXFORD

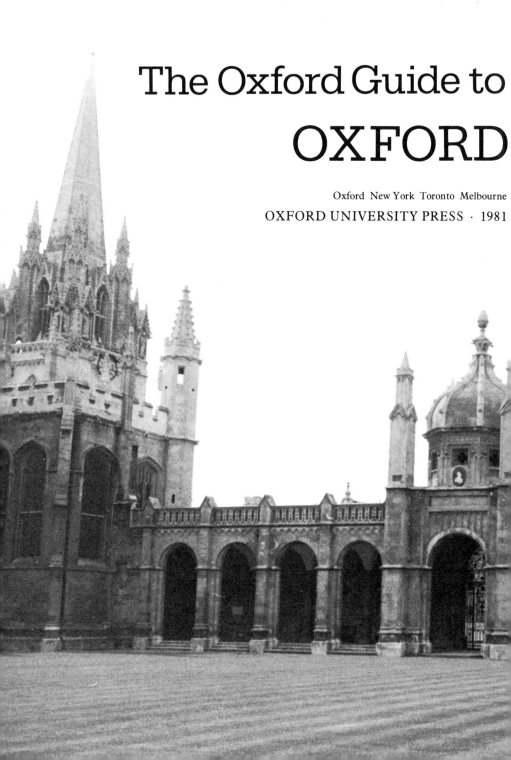

The Oxford Guide to
OXFORD

Oxford New York Toronto Melbourne
OXFORD UNIVERSITY PRESS · 1981

PETER HEYWORTH

WITH PHOTOGRAPHS BY

HUNTER CORDAIY

TO OXFORD
w.a.f.
and to Elspeth who has none

Oxford University Press, Walton Street, Oxford OX2 6DP

London Glasgow New York Toronto
Delhi Bombay Calcutta Madras Karachi
Kuala Lumpur Singapore Hong Kong Tokyo
Nairobi Dar es Salaam Cape Town
Melbourne Wellington
and associated companies in
Beirut Berlin Ibadan Mexico City

British Library Cataloguing in Publication Data

Heyworth, Peter Lorriman
The Oxford guide to Oxford.
1. Oxford – Description – Guide-books
I. Title
914.25'74'04857   DA690.098   80-40807
ISBN 0-19-211581-2
ISBN 0-19-285095-4 pbk

Typeset by Oxprint Ltd, Oxford
and printed in Great Britain by
Lowe & Brydone Printers Limited,
Thetford, Norfolk

Title-page photograph: Radcliffe Camera from All Souls College, with Hawksmoor's arcade, gatehouse, and cupola, and the University Church of St Mary the Virgin on the left

Prefatory note

There can be no justification for adding to the existing stock of Oxford guides so I will not attempt to offer one here. My purpose has been to celebrate the visual delights of the place, of the Oxford that the visitor actually encounters, and I have for the most part included potted history and anecdote only where it helps to explain what the eye actually sees. The exceptions are self-indulgent, but I find it hard to apologize for Mrs Jeune of Pembroke, or Dr Newton of Hertford, or Robert de Eglesfield, Founder of Queen's – who has in any case sentimental claims on me as a fellow West Cumbrian.

I have tried to avoid received opinions and comfortable orthodoxies. I have tried to see things as they are, to respond to one thing at a time, individually, and to set down what I saw and understood. Over a period of three weeks in the late summer of 1979 I looked at all but a handful of the places described here – often for the hundredth time – occasionally for the first time. I have denied myself the pleasure of second looks and, except in a few cases, second thoughts. Perhaps it would have been a better book if I had not, but I do not think so.

I have followed the convention in books of this kind of not acknowledging sources. Those familiar with the literature will have no difficulty in identifying the books I have used, and I do not hesitate to say how grateful I am for the industry of Anthony Wood and Tom Hearne, Rashdall and Pantin, Pevsner and the inspectors of the Royal Commission on Historical Monuments, Wells and Morris, and dozens of others, and for the help and pleasure they have given me.

Hugo Brunner gave me the opportunity to write this guide and it fell to Hilary Dickinson, Susan le Roux, and Bob Elliott to make a book out of it. Hunter Cordaiy took the photographs and I confess I believe the better part to be his. To them and to everyone else who had a hand in it I am deeply grateful.

P.L.H.

Toronto
April 1980

Contents

What to see   8

Places to eat   9

Pubs   10

Public lavatories   11

Near Oxford   12

Books to read   14

GAZETEER   17

Index   153

Maps   157

What to see

To spend less than a week in Oxford is an exercise in frustration but mc
people do, so these itineraries are governed by what is best to see, and wh
can best be seen, in the time available, and with apologies for the om
sions.

HALF A DAY   New College, St Edmund Hall, Magdalen College, Botanic Garden,
Mary the Virgin, seen in that order.

ONE DAY   Morning: Trinity College, Wadham College, Sheldonian Theatre, Bo
leian Library, Divinity School, Brasenose College, Lincoln Colleg
Afternoon: New College, St Edmund Hall, Magdalen College, Botan
Garden, St Mary the Virgin, seen in that order.

TWO DAYS   The first day as ONE DAY above. The second day, morning: Christ Churc
Oriel College, Corpus Christi College, Merton College, Merton Fields, ar
Christ Church Meadow. Afternoon: St Catherine's College, Mansfie
College, University Museum and Pitt Rivers Museum, Keble Colleg
University Parks, Worcester College, seen in that order.

A WEEK   Best spent taking the two-day itinerary in a more leisurely way ar
revisiting what takes the fancy first time round. Add the Queen's Colleg
St John's College, St Anne's College, Wolfson College, and the Ashmole
Museum – which needs a full day to itself. Outings to Binsey, Wytha
Iffley, and Old Headington. In summer, punting, preferably on the Che
well from Cherwell Boathouse, and walking the Thames tow-path south
Iffley Lock (beginning at Folly Bridge) and north to Binsey and Godst
(beginning at Walton Well Road).

Other manageable walks are along the Cherwell north to the Victo
Arms at Marston Ferry, south through St Catherine's and Magdal
Colleges, both starting from the University Parks gate opposite Keb
College, and, for the more energetic, Shotover Common can be reach
across Magdalen Bridge and via St Clement's, Headington Hill, Chen
Lane, Old Road, to Shotover.

Places to eat

Starting at the top, so to speak, the Elizabeth (84 St Aldate's. tel. 42230) has had a reputation for imaginative cooking for nearly thirty years and at its best can be very good indeed. La Sorbonne (130a High Street – down an alley-way east of Carfax, tel. 41320) offers the best French cooking in the area; and if 'atmosphere' is important a meal here affords the pleasure of eating in a seventeenth-century house (originally called Kemp Hall) authentic inside as well as out. (La Sorbonne has a modest annexe, Casse Croûte, open for lunches only.) The Randolph Hotel (Beaumont Street) is a Trust House Forte hotel with the usual pretensions and a grand dining-room. Also, in Summertown (272 Banbury Road, tel. 53540), Les Quat' Saisons, which was the only restaurant to be awarded two stars in the 1980 Egon Ronay Guide. All of these are expensive.

Decent meals at reasonable prices are not easy to find. A simple and well-cooked meal (dinners only) in a lovely setting can be got at the Cherwell Boathouse (tel. 55978) – it lies on the bank of the Cherwell just off Bardwell Road (itself off the Banbury Road) and so is a bit remote. So is the Luna Caprese (Italian, 4 North Parade, tel. 54812), but worth the effort.

For lunches there are a number of more or less brisk places, more or less alike (as their names suggest), listed here by area. Nearest the centre, The Nose Bag (6–8 St Michael's Street), Bevers (36 St Michael's Street), Pippins (8 Ship Street); further out, off St Giles', Brown's Restaurant (7 Woodstock Road at Little Clarendon Street), Quincey's (10 Little Clarendon Street). Most of the pubs listed below serve standard pub food at lunchtime.

There are a dozen Indian restaurants and a dozen Chinese, all very hit and miss. The Indian places are concentrated in two neighbourhoods at opposite ends of Oxford, Walton Street and Cowley Road. The Taj Mahal is central (16 Turl Street) and has been thought well of since the Second World War.

If your taste stretches to what the steak-house chains have to offer try the Mitre (High Street) and the Golden Cross (Cornmarket), two old coaching inns which sold out.

Pubs

There are, or were in 1978, 168 active pubs in Oxford and neighbourhoo
Paul Marriott lists them in his useful little book *Oxford Pubs Past a*
Present, and in the course of duty he visited them all. The student pub
cation *The Oxford Handbook* has a consumers' survey of pubs in Oxfo
and surrounding villages.

What follows is a summary list arranged broadly by areas since the be
pubs after a day spent grafting round monuments are those nearest t
place you happen to find yourself. Those marked with an asterisk a
especially agreeable.

CARFAX The Bulldog (St Aldate's) is a big, brisk, town pub, the Apollo (St Aldate'
is Edwardian pastiche and friendly. The Wheatsheaf and Chequers★ bo
lie in yards behind the High Street between Carfax and King Edwa
Street; the Wheatsheaf is a town pub and a bit short on charm, t
Chequers was a nice old place with authentic medieval outcroppings in t
bar, now renovated. The Bear★ (Bear Lane) is tiny, quaint, and usual
overfull. The Crown and the Corn Dolly (both just off the Cornmarket) a
roughish – the Crown serves heavy rock on tape with its beer, the Co
Dolly is subterranean and serves its rock live, nightly. The St Micha
Tavern (St Michael's Street) serves Real Ale on three floors.

WESTGATE Not much has survived the bulldozers but the Royal Blenheim (St Ebbe
is a solid pub which takes food seriously enough to provide separate tab
and tablecloths; the Westgate (Bonn Square) offers no frills.

GLOUCESTER GREEN The Welsh Pony (George Street) is charmless but was the first pub to ser
(Bus Station) food in Oxford (*c*.1950) and still charges 1970 prices. The Grape
(George Street) is Victorian pastiche and pretty well done. The Glouces
Arms (Friars' Entry) and the Red Lion (Gloucester Green) survive
theatrical pubs even though the theatre on the whole hasn't.

ST GILES' Lamb and Flag (St Giles'), long and narrow with a remote juke-box. T
Eagle and Child (St Giles') chintzy and a bit genteel – C. S. Lewis, J. R.
Tolkein, and cronies used to drink there. Duke of Cambridge★ (Lit
Clarendon Street) a cosy one-room pub with an unexpected rustic arbc
behind.

BODLEIAN Turf Tavern★ (St Helen's Passage, off New College Lane), Oxford's me
celebrated pub, hard to find, and a bit of a squeeze, but good value and
atmospheric garden in summer. The Kings Arms (corner of Broad Stre

and Holywell), a concourse of bustling bars serving food energetically most of the day. White Horse* (Broad Street at Blackwell's), small and friendly.

For the punter Head of the River (Folly Bridge), big, impersonal, animated. Going north on the Thames is the Watermans Arms at Osney, going south the Isis* at Iffley Lock. On the further reaches of the Cherwell at Marston Ferry Road, the Victoria Arms.

Country pubs easily accessible by car The Perch* (Binsey), White Hart* (Wytham), Trout (Godstow), Kings Arms* (Sandford-on-Thames), the Fishes* (North Hinksey).

Pubs with gardens or parents with children Turf Tavern*, Chequers*, in the town; outside, the Perch* (Binsey), Trout (Godstow), White Hart* (Wytham), the Fishes* (North Hinksey), Kings Arms* (Sandford-on-Thames), and all the riverside pubs listed above.

Public lavatories

The big municipal set pieces are in St Giles' opposite the Martyrs' Memorial, Blue Boar Street just off St Aldate's, and near Folly Bridge at the corner of St Aldate's and Thames Street – new, salubrious, and with special provision for the disabled. Nearest to the centre of things is the lavatory in Market Street, off the Cornmarket.

Lavatories inside the University Museum and the Ashmolean Museum, and in the quadrangle of the Bodleian Library (but this is for men only, and is heavily disguised as the 'Schola Linguarum Hebraicae et Graecae'), are only usable when the buildings are open.

Remote sites are those on the Banbury Road at Park Town; St Bernard's Road (men only) next to the Horse and Jockey (69 Woodstock Road); York Place (St Clement's) across Magdalen Bridge; at the Cherwell Boathouse (off Chadlington Road); in the University Parks beside the Cricket Pavilion, accessible from the Keble Gate, and (men only) in the enclosure at Parsons' Pleasure, accessible from the gate at the corner of South Parks Road and St Cross Road.

The larger shops (for example, Debenhams) afford relief during business hours as, of course, do pubs and restaurants. There are lavatories at the Bus Station (Gloucester Green) and the Railway Station. Porters at college lodges can be helpful.

Near Oxford

One of the pleasures of Oxford is that it is easy to escape from it t
surrounding countryside and neighbouring counties offering constar
small, and occasional immoderate, delights. What is listed here is for thos
who want some relief from collegiate architecture and urban business
Refreshment is the chief consideration, and also accounts for what ha
been omitted, and in particular the omission of the monumental and th
overpeopled.

The best places lie west and north of Oxford; there Oxfordshire run
away into neighbouring Berkshire, Gloucestershire, and Warwickshir
where those counties are at their loveliest. A car and a good road map ar
necessary, a road map which distinguishes 'A' class roads from the rest, fc
the rule is to get off the 'A' roads as soon as possible and to hold to 'B' road
and to roads of no class at all. Places are listed with the town from whic
they are most easily accessible.

ABINGDON A proud Thames-side town 9 kilometres (6 miles) south of Oxford wit
handsome municipal buildings and churches, and the ruins of a grea
Benedictine abbey. DORCHESTER (9 kilometres – 6 miles – east of Abing
don) has a surviving abbey church with the finest mix of medieval glass an
sculpture in the county. East again (6 kilometres: 4 miles) EWELME has
good group of church (with Chaucer family monuments) and almshouses
The direct route back to Oxford from Ewelme via Stadhampton is throug
pretty, pottering country full of thatch and village greens.

FARINGDON A rambling country town 27 kilometres (17 miles) west of Oxford muc
distressed by a one-way traffic system. At GREAT COXWELL (3 kilometres
2 miles – south-west) is the only surviving Cistercian barn in England sti
in use – a cathedral of a place. Further south, just beyond UFFINGTON
White Horse Hill, an ancient pagan monument cut into the chalk of th
escarpment on the north side of an immense Iron Age earthwork known a
Uffington Castle with superb views over the Vale of White Horse. Betwee
them runs the Ridgeway, an ancient road which follows the edge of th
escarpment. Three kilometres (2 miles) west along the Ridgeway Wa
land's Smithy, a long barrow with burial chambers. The Thames can b
crossed at Radcot Bridge to reach KELMSCOTT; William Morris lived in th
manor for twenty-five years (it is still occasionally viewable) and is burie
in the churchyard. INGLESHAM 3 kilometres (2 miles) west is a lone
Norman church in a farmyard, saved by Morris from the Victorian res
torers. West again, FAIRFORD with its incomparable stained glass. East c
Faringdon just off the Oxford road is PUSEY HOUSE with romantic an
usually underpopulated gardens.

1

BURFORD   West of Oxford (30 kilometres: 19 miles) still keeps its character despite traffic, tourists, and antique shops, and gives access to the valley of the RIVER WINDRUSH. SWINBROOK (3 kilometres: 2 miles) in particular is worth a visit, with its church stacked with tombs of the Fettiplace family; and beyond it a short distance over the fields WIDFORD church, without a village but with Roman mosaic (originally a Roman villa stood on the site), medieval wall paintings, and nineteenth-century box pews. MINSTER LOVELL further down the valley is a picturesque but dispirited place with a romantic fifteenth-century manorial ruin beside the Windrush. South-east of Burford (8 kilometres: 5 miles) BAMPTON a spacious country town with a very grand church visible for miles and, as often as not, Morris dancing in the streets on public holidays in the summer months. West of Bampton (5 kilometres: 3 miles) a pretty group of villages – LANGFORD, BROADWELL, and KENCOT – all with good churches, and all different. The Norman sculpture of the Crucifixion over the south porch of Langford church is worth going a long way to see. NORTHLEACH lies west of Burford on the Cheltenham road and has a sumptuous fifteenth-century 'wool' church. South-west of Northleach CHEDWORTH – Roman villa, more or less intact – and BIBURY, almshouses, fishponds, and tourists galore.

CHIPPING NORTON   North-west of Oxford (30 kilometres: 19 miles). A bustling market town. GREAT TEW to the north-east (8 kilometres: 5 miles) is a nineteenth-century model village now a bit decayed, but an extraordinary essay in the pictur-esque. GREAT ROLLRIGHT (3 kilometres – 2 miles – north of Chipping Norton) has a stone circle, an unusually primitive touch for this part of the world. Beyond that (1½ kilometres: 1 mile) lies HOOK NORTON, a famous brewery with a village attached. North-west of Chipping Norton on the Moreton road CHASTLETON HOUSE, brooding, Jacobean, untouched by charm. This road followed through Moreton-in-Marsh leads to CHIPPING CAMPDEN (24 kilometres: 15 miles), loveliest and least assertive of the authentic Cotswold wool towns, and to one of England's jewels – HIDCOTE MANOR GARDENS – near by.

BANBURY   North of Oxford (35 kilometres: 22 miles) has its cross (modern) and a massive, imperious, imperial church described at the time of its construc-tion (1800) as 'more like a gaol than a Christian temple', and in orange stone at that. BROUGHTON CASTLE (3 kilometres – 2 miles – south-west), medi-eval, moated, marvellous. BLOXHAM, ADDERBURY, and DEDDINGTON with spectacular village churches, stand together just south of BANBURY. Returning to Oxford, just off the main road 8 kilometres (5 miles) south of Deddington, ROUSHAM HOUSE preserves an eighteenth-century landscaped park by William Kent which runs along the River Cherwell.

13

East of Oxford (19 kilometres: 12 miles) has an immensely wide main stree⟨ full of good domestic architecture of all periods, and a fine church. RYCOT⟩ (6½ kilometres – 4 miles – south-west) is a perfectly preserve⟨ seventeenth-century chapel with a theatrical presence, and a house, but n⟨ village, near by. A pretty route back to Oxford runs through BRILL on it⟨ hill, STUDLEY, BECKLEY, and ELSFIELD.

Books to read

The two outstanding general accounts, quite different from each other, Jan Morris's *Oxford* (1978) and Felix Markham's *Oxford* (1975). Morris's i⟨ the best sort of journalism, written with her customary panache. Markha⟨ provides an elegant and thoughtful survey of the University from it⟨ beginnings; he has the advantage of brilliantly atmospheric photograph⟨ by Penny Tweedie – it is really half her book.

For buildings the bible is, of course, Nikolaus Pevsner's account of th⟨ University and city in the *Oxfordshire* volume of the great Pevsner⟨ Penguin enterprise The Buildings of England (1974); the photographs ar⟨ as usual too few and too muddy but there is still nothing to match it. Th⟨ best photographic record is in the Royal Commission on Historical Mon⟨ ments volume *The City of Oxford* (1939), but this, like all RCHM volume⟨ treats nothing after 1714. For post-1714 there are good photographs i⟨ David Hinton's *Oxford Buildings, From Medieval to Modern* (exteriors only⟨ photographed by David Carpenter) published by the Oxford Archaeolog⟨ cal Excavation Committee (1972) – which has also published an interes⟨ ting record (by T. G. Hassall) of recent excavations, especially those mad⟨ possible by new commercial developments in the Cornmarket and in S⟨ Ebbe's for the Westgate Centre, *Oxford: The City Beneath Your Fe⟨* (1972). For buildings after 1960 there are excellent photographs in *Ne⟨ Architecture in Oxford* by David Reed and Philip Opher (1977).

The authoritative historical account is vol. III of the Victoria History c⟨ the County of Oxford: *The University of Oxford* (1954).

A survey of the University is provided in the semi-official *Handbook ⟨ the University of Oxford* (1967 and later) – part i has a series of chapter⟨ describing the University and all its activities, part ii is a detailed guide t⟨ the rules and regulations of the University. *The Oxford Handboo⟨* (annually) is student compiled and student oriented – a useful rag-bag c⟨ information, listing undergraduate clubs, societies, and services and offe⟨ ing surveys of restaurants, pubs, shops, entertainment, etc.

1

There are countless tourist guides. The most reliable is A. R. Woolley, *The Clarendon Guide to Oxford* (1979). A series of pamphlets by Malcolm Graham designed for those who choose to explore the city (as distinct from the University) on foot, are issued under the auspices of the Local History Section of the Central Library; the city is divided into areas with a pamphlet on each, full of information and nicely matter of fact.

A guide of a sort and the most entertaining thing of its kind is John Betjeman's *Oxford University Chest* (1979 but a straight reprint of the book of 1938), a period piece full of engaging prejudices but always illuminating as well as funny. It has lots of grainy, evocative photographs of the thirties by Maholy-Nagy. Not, however, for those who want facts, straight and unvarnished.

The best map is Alden's *Pocket Street Plan to Oxford*. Among the usual run-of-the-mill commercial stuff, outstanding postcards are those of Edwin Smith published by Gordon Fraser, but unfortunately not easy to find. Postcards from historical photographs in the John Johnson collection in the Bodleian Library are on sale at the bookstall in the Bodleian.

Gazeteer

Map references below headings refer to the Inner Oxford map (pages 158–9). Places without references will be found on the Outer Oxford map (page 157).

ABINGDON ROAD   Follows the line of the Grand Pont, an immense causeway built in the late twelfth century to carry the road to the south over the marshes between Folly Bridge and Hinksey Hill; as a result the Abingdon Road is still markedly higher than the surrounding land. The swampiness of the terrain made settlement impossible and the area remained undeveloped until the opening of the Great Western Railway Station just south of Folly Bridge in 1844.

ALFRED STREET   A narrow cobbled street off the High opposite St Mary the Virgin. The
7C   modern front of St Columba's church (1960) conceals an interior of 1916.

ALL SAINTS   A stylish church and unusual in Oxford for that. Large, high, and open as
6C   was the fashion in early eighteenth-century preaching churches, designed for good viewing and easy listening. Everything is forceful: the two ranges of wrap-around windows, the balustrading, and especially the strong tower with its striking long-necked spire. The west end of the High Street would be a very poor place without it. No longer used as a church but as a library for Lincoln College, with an imaginatively remodelled interior.

ALL SOULS   All Souls is, like St Antony's and Nuffield, a college for graduate members
COLLEGE   only. It was founded in 1438, by Henry Chichele, Archbishop of Canter-
6D   bury, and in its name 'The College of All Souls of the Faithful Departed' it was intended especially to celebrate those who fell in the wars for the Crown of France, the so-called Hundred Years War.

   The Front Quad opening off the High Street is claustrophobic, which is a great shock especially if approached from the buoyant spaces of Radcliff Square. It is also dirty in a way that anyone who knew Oxford before 195 will feel at home with, and may, not wholly sentimentally, feel the loss of Like an old photograph it validates memory and one is thankful in the renewed, smoothed, scrubbed Oxford for that. Built 1438–43, after New College and before Magdalen, it is quite unlike either.

   The chapel, with its sudden approach up a dark, blind alley-way, fill the north side. It has had a troubled history and survival has been haphazard business. The Protestant Visitors of Edward VI attacked it with a studied violence in 1549; the carved figures of the great stone reredo were smashed and the reredos lay in ruins for a century, and at the same time the organ was torn out. The chapel plate and vestments were destroyed in the sixteenth century as too Popish; the fifteenth-century misericords survived but the stalls have Victorian tops. The reredos was plastered up in 1664 and painted with a sprawling Last Judgement by Isaac Fuller the Oxford painter (who is said to have 'dissipated his talents with ignoble indulgences', meaning he drank too much); John Evelyn didn't care for it – he thought it 'too full of nakeds for a college chapel' – and neither apparently did the Fellows for it was replaced in 1714 by a painting of the resurrection of the Founder by Sir James Thornhill. The ceiling was panelled in 1664 and it was also painted by Fuller. Both reredos and roo

Opposite: New Hinksey,
238 Abingdon Road

were discovered in 1870 and restored – remnants of Fuller's ceiling panels hang in the antechapel. Some of the fifteenth-century floor tiles have survived (the rest of the floor is seventeenth century) and so has most of the fifteenth-century glass of the antechapel. The cloister on the north side was demolished in 1703.

So there remains a gorgeous reredos seething with ornament and so animated that its figures seem about to step out from their niches to greet you; much excellent glass; and a wooden screen (1664, altered 1716) painted black and gold, with ceilings carried on pillars and a great arch between – it is of great character, rather like a small temple. A chapel that should be memorable yet what the memory preserves is a depressed image of discoloured stone and tarnished gilt. Disconsolate is the word. Do the Fellows of All Souls love it? Perhaps they do not: they have never replaced the organ.

North Quad is a much more cheerful place and we have the Gothic fantasies of Nicholas Hawksmoor to thank for that. Hawksmoor, of course, is more often judged from outside his quadrangle than from within it since only his famous towers are prominent from Radcliffe Square and the surrounding area and they are very prominent indeed. But his quadrangle is much less excited than is commonly believed, and standing on the south side between chapel and hall it shows itself to be altogether the controlled composition that Hawksmoor obviously intended it to be. The two towers are a powerful centre-piece of a long symmetrical range with three tiers of expressive, deep-set windows; and if only his pinnacles with their ball-and-flower ornament are 'correct' Gothic, then archaeology must suffer that art may be served.

The cloister range opposite owes nothing to Gothic; a single arcade, precise in its rhythm, with its own centre-piece – a gatehouse with cupola and not at all competitive with Hawksmoor's towers or Gibbs's Radcliffe Camera. Fine wrought-iron gates also to Hawksmoor's design let on to Radcliffe Square. In the bays of the cloister are hung large hatchments – colourful fossils of an All Souls tradition that the coats of arms of Wardens who die in office are displayed for a year after their death.

The north side is filled by the great mass of the Codrington Library (1715–40), built to a cathedral-like scale, and entered in the usual understated Oxford manner by a small door at the north end of the cloister. There is nothing understated about the inside: it is a single vast room nearly 60 metres (200 ft) long and monumentally wasteful of space – a self-indulgence that Hawksmoor persuaded James Gibbs to emulate in his library design for the Radcliffe Camera. Codrington marks a decisive break from the medieval stall system (still in use at Queen's twenty years earlier) to a wall system; and it gave to the University what is unquestionably its noblest space and to Oxford the conundrum of a building wholly 'Gothic' in its exterior details and wholly 'classical' within.

Hawksmoor's quadrangle is completed by his hall built in 1730, replacing the fifteenth-century building, and altogether in a lower key than the

ll Saints churchyard,
asenose College, and the
ire of St Mary the Virgin

21

rest of his work. Next to the hall on the east is the buttery with a gorgeous plaster ceiling dramatically lit.

The sundial high on Codrington's south front is thought to have been designed by Sir Christopher Wren when he was bursar of All Souls; it is so accurate that in the words of a Victorian guidebook 'before the days of telegraphic communication, the Oxford watchmakers used to set their clocks by it'. It is a reminder that the whole quadrangle shows best in the sharp sunlight of early morning or late afternoon: John Betjeman points out that Hawksmoor's towers are designed for shadows.

The fine house at the east end of the High Street front is the Warden's Lodgings and probably the earliest piece of Palladian architecture in England.

ANGEL AND GREYHOUND MEADOWS
7E

Lying beneath Magdalen Bridge on the north side, lush, green, and inviting still, they are reminders of two ancient inns for which the meadows supplied hay and grazing for horses.

The Angel was the fashionable Oxford inn of the seventeenth century and Anthony Wood catalogues the grandees (ambassadors and the like) who put up there. In 1651 Wood tells how Jacob a Jew opened a coffee house there and 'it was by some, who delighted in noveltie, drank'. In the nineteenth century it was a busy coaching inn; in its kitchens in 1874 Mrs Frank Cooper made the first 'Oxford' marmalade – affectionately known to undergraduates of the time as 'Squishy'. It made for itself a reputation in the world and one it still has.

The Angel was demolished to make way for the Examination Schools in the 1880s (though part of it can still be seen above no. 84 High Street), and the Greyhound, which stood at the corner of Longwall and High Street, in 1851.

ARISTOTLE LANE
1A

Named after Aristotle's Well, now concealed in the basement of a near-by building; it gives access to Port Meadow north of the city centre and offers good views of the canal north and south where it bridges it.

ASHMOLEAN MUSEUM
5B

The history of Oxford's institutions is full of improbable origins and fortunate accidents but the most engaging story of all is that which traces the splendid collections of the Ashmolean Museum back to a seventeenth-century Suffolk gardener with no sense of smell, who wrote the first account of Russian plants after a voyage to Archangel and later spent seven months on an expedition against Algerian pirates. He ended his career as Keeper of the Royal Gardens, Vines, and Silkworms to Charles I and Henrietta Maria, and with his son (also a gardener and traveller) was responsible for introducing into English gardens the lilac, evening primrose, night-scented stock, Virginia creeper, the passion-flower, red dogwood, the Dutch medlar, the wild pomegranate, stag's horn sumach, acacia, the wild tulip tree, and the parents of the London plane tree which was developed as a hybrid in Oxford thirty years after his death.

This was John Tradescant (died 1638). His curiosity and acquisitiveness were not restricted to flowers and plants, and in his travels he amassed large collections of chiefly natural historical and anthropological interest which, in his last years, were exhibited in his house in Lambeth. This celebrated collection – popularly known as 'Tradescant's Ark' – was augmented by his son John the Younger (1608–62) and bequeathed by him to Elias Ashmole (1617–92), the Oxford antiquary, in 1659. Ashmole in his turn offered the collection to the University on condition that the University made provision for housing it; and this condition being met by the construction of a new building (the Old Ashmolean) near the Bodleian Library, Ashmole despatched the 'Ark' from London in twelve carts and the Ashmolean Museum, the oldest public museum in England and one of the oldest in Europe, was opened on 21 May 1683.

The present building was completed in 1845 to the designs of C. R. Cockerell (1788–1863) who won a competition to provide under one roof accommodation for the University picture and sculpture galleries (which had been housed since Sir Thomas Bodley's time in the Bodleian Library) and for an institute to be devoted to the teaching of modern languages, the gift of Sir Robert Taylor in 1788. The Taylorian, as it is commonly known, occupies the range which faces on to St Giles', the Ashmolean (with extensions of 1894, 1932, 1937–40, and 1959–61) the rest.

'Neo-classical' describes well enough a design which owes something to the Temple of Apollo at Bassae. Grecian, that is, but as always with Cockerell independent – as in the daring way he sets the portico and adjacent façade with its restrained emphasis of fluted columns, rams-horn capitals, shallow pilasters, and plain stone panels with wreaths carved on them, between two powerful, projecting, and higher wings articulated by a double range of strong windows, the strength reinforced by the sculptural depth of the protruding columns crowned with urns, their upward thrust carried beyond the high attic range by prominent chimneys. It could have been a deadly embrace, but it isn't.

Towards St Giles', which is the front of the Taylorian, the design is identical except that the columns are detached and, instead of urns, carry statues of France, Italy, Germany, and Spain, like the other excellent carving, by W. G. Nicholl, who later did good work in Worcester chapel. Although the Taylorian is one wing of two in the larger composition it is a convincing achievement in its own right, with nothing to contradict its forcefulness. Cockerell thought of it as 'something of a tribute to the memory of Nicholas Hawksmoor'.

The interior of the museum is surprisingly intimate and while it has its share of brocaded walls and ornate gilt there is remarkable variety in the displays, constituting in themselves a museum of museum fashions. A few, like the Leeds Room (Roman and Anglo-Saxon antiquities) and the John Evans Room (Prehistoric Europe), are agreeably cluttered in the nineteenth-century manner; others, like the Beazley Room (Greek antiquities), represent the best modern standards of elegantly displayed

24

art, in the case of the Department of Eastern Art, seductively lit.

The most satisfying exhibit, a work of art in itself, is also the most remote – the last of the three galleries on the top floor, and the terminus of the museum, so to speak. It consists of three small interconnecting rooms housing the Ward Bequest, a collection of Dutch and Flemish still-life paintings arranged with exquisite judgement in a setting of sympathetic pieces – a seventeenth-century brass writing table with tortoise-shell inlay, a fifteenth-century South German group representing the Adoration of the Magi, carved out of pear wood, a number of fine carved wooden chests, a collection of seventeenth- and eighteenth-century English glass, and measuring the time in this timeless spot a splendid long case clock of c.1720 by Joseph Williams of London. With its cool white walls and black-and-white diapered floor the scene is like a Vermeer come to life.

What is not to be missed? Piero di Cosimo's *Forest Fire*, and the memory of Sir Henry Channon's account of standing before it, moved to see again a picture which had long hung in his rooms, and wondering why he ever let it leave them; *Le Messie* (The Messiah), a Stradivarius in matchless condition, enjoyed for the incongruity of merely viewing what above all one would like to hear but which no one is allowed to play; the Egyptian fertility god Min, brooding in the darkness of the Griffith Gallery; the University Chest; Edward Pierce's bust of Sir Christopher Wren and Roubiliac's of G. F. Handel; Samuel Palmer's visionary Shoreham paintings, their mystical enthusiasm reverently veiled by a roller-blind; the collection of French nineteenth-century paintings – by Pissarro, Courbet, Corot, Cézanne – which show the more brilliantly beside the vulgar Pre-Raphaelite posturing next door; John William Inchbold's *A Study in March*, exemplifying Swinburne's lines about him – 'To thee the sun spake, and the morning sang/Notes deep and clear as life or heaven' Finally, and not for piety's sake, Powhatan's Mantle, the ceremonial cloak given by Chief Powhatan, father of Pocahontas, to Captain Christopher Newport in 1608 and already in Tradescant's collection by 1631: the earliest North American Indian garment to survive, the earliest example of American abstract art, and a masterpiece.

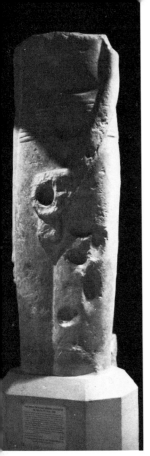

Above: Egyptian fertility god Min, Ashmolean Museum

Opposite: Ward Bequest, Ashmolean Museum

BALLIOL COLLEGE
6C

Balliol's fame is great but not of very long standing. In 1674 Humphrey Prideaux, who admittedly didn't think much of anybody, reported on Balliol men who 'by perpetual bubbing add art to their natural stupidity, to make themselves perfect sots'. That is no doubt a coloured account (Prideaux wasn't sure whether to believe it himself) but if it is not wholly remote from the truth it helps explain why any list of Balliol's 'famous men' is bottom heavy with names from the nineteenth and twentieth centuries. The story of Balliol's renaissance (in the early nineteenth century at least coupled with Oriel) which carried an often reluctant University in its wake is well known. The abolition of tied fellowships and the establishment of open scholarships; the requirement to read for an Honours degree; the

establishment of a tutorial system; and the encouragement of science wit'
the opening of a chemistry laboratory in conjunction with Trinity.

Balliol's buildings are less easy to praise than its recent history. It :
not to be expected that the fabric would be spared the college's lust fc
reform and needless to say it wasn't. Its present buildings date with two (
three exceptions from the nineteenth century. The best architects wer
employed: Waterhouse, the Broad Street front and the hall; Butterfielc
the chapel; Salvin, the library tower and part of the St Giles' front – th(
rest of which has bits by later nineteenth-century architects, G. Basevi an(
E. P. Warren. And all were capable of much better work than Balliol gc
from them.

Waterhouse's Broad Street façade is the most distinctive – a façad(
assertive enough to deter the faint-hearted from going beyond it. In fact th(
pretensions do not last long. The Front Quad has an almost intimate air
markedly so if the spectator keeps his back to Waterhouse's two rang(
(south and east). The west range (the old hall), and the north range left (
the passage way facing the lodge (the old library), are the only mediev;
buildings remaining, united as a new library. Butterfield's chapel (
1856–7 was built before Waterhouse's ranges (1867–8) and befor
Butterfield discovered the pleasures of exploring Oxford's tolerances in h
design for Keble (1868–82), and just as well. He took his scale from th(
medieval hall and library, and on Broad Street the fifteenth-century gat(
tower and eighteenth-century work adjacent to it swept away by Water
house ten years later. The result is broad, low, and dull, with an interior fc
which Butterfield isn't to blame. It was redone very timidly in 1937 nc
long after Merton had remodelled and reduced to anonymity Butterfield
Grove Building. What did the thirties have against him? Post-war Balli(
must bear responsibility for the four large space-heaters which look lik(
four large space-heaters and disfigure the central aisle.

Salvin's tower (1853) in the angle of the library gives access to Garde
Quad. The range to the left (south-west corner) has a happily settled lool
it is by Henry Keene, 1767. From this the quadrangle stretches in a(
L-shape north to Waterhouse's new hall, 1876–7. It is, it must be said,
very dispiriting place. It can make up its mind neither what it wants to d(
nor what it is supposed to be, and the succession of its buildings, 171(
1826–7, 1912–13, 1852, 1907, going north are as dislocated as the chro(
ology suggests. The whole range has an aimless continuity; uncertainty (
purpose is the last thing one would expect of Balliol but uncertain(
of purpose here cannot be denied.

The hall is in the centre of the short arm of the L: very high with
hall-high undercroft and a grand staircase. Inside the organ in the gallery
a real monument where the rest of the hall attempts monumentality an
fails. Run-of-the-mill portraits, one of the famous Victorian Mast(
Benjamin Jowett hanging rather surprisingly in the wings. The hall
flanked by new buildings of 1965 and 1968 which only Sir John Betjema
could do justice to.

Balliol is not a college to encourage antiquarianism but very creditably they have salvaged the original college gates offered for sale as firewood when Waterhouse dismantled the Broad Street front in 1867 and then bought by a Magdalen man (who declared it a pity that gates which had witnessed judicial burnings at the stake set up opposite them in Broad Street should themselves end up in flames) and removed to Nelmes in Essex. They were returned to the college in 1926 and hang in the archway beneath Salvin's library tower.

BANBURY ROAD   Its character is very largely lost as a result of University development in the south and commercial development north to Summertown (South Parade) and beyond, but it gives access to much of interest: the University Parks, North Parade, Park Town, Cherwell Boathouse, Wolfson College, and three of the women's colleges – St Anne's, Lady Margaret Hall, and St Hugh's south to north in that order.

BATH PLACE
6D   Pretty composition of pastel cottages round a sloping cobbled courtyard opening off Holywell towards the Turf Tavern.

BEAR LANE
7C   Overlain by the back of Christ Church's Peckwater Quad which fills the south side. On the north Lincoln College's new Quatermaine's Building on the site of the former Quatermaine's Stables, but in between times occupied by the Bear Lane Gallery which for twenty years cheerfully sustained the cause of modern art in a city indifferent to it.

BEAUMONT BUILDINGS
5B   A single untidy brick terrace of early nineteenth-century artisans' houses beside which the British Council Offices (J. G. Fryman, 1966–7), all fins like a prototype radiator, look very much at home.

BEAUMONT STREET
5B   It begins fortissimo at St Giles' with the Ashmolean Museum and the Randolph Hotel, then subsides into four terraces of handsome Georgian stone houses (laid out 1828–37 on the site of Beaumont Palace), many with balconies, some canopied, and completed by the front of Worcester College which stops it at the west end.

BINSEY   A handful of cottages, a farm, a pub, a few muddy puddles, and a church, Binsey is a remote place set in fields on the banks of the Thames; it is hard to believe that it is barely 3 kilometres (2 miles) from the centre of Oxford by car (via Binsey Lane), and less than that on foot through Port Meadow and the tow-path towards Godstow.

The church, dedicated to St Margaret of Antioch, lies at the dead end of Binsey Lane a short distance beyond the village; it has Norman dog-tooth and zigzag and a tub-shaped Norman font, mixed and rather faded glass in the east window, and an immense eighteenth-century hatchment. Inside the pulpit is, apparently, a carving of St Frideswide by Eric Gill, accounted too strong for public display. Flagged floor, oil lamps, and its pervasive

29

Red brick at Oxford,
Beaumont Buildings

dampness encourage the romantic air appropriate to a church which had its beginnings in a saintly miracle. St Frideswide, a Saxon princess in her own right, retreated here from Oxford to escape a suitor; he followed her and, insistent in his demands, was struck blind. St Frideswide in her compassion prayed to St Margaret and was ordered to strike the ground with her staff; the water which gushed out restored the sight of the amorous suitor. The Holy Well lies just to the west of the church and in the Middle Ages was a place of popular pilgrimage, reputed to be especially efficacious in the cure of eye diseases, indigestion, and infertility. Nicholas Breakspear (c.1100–59), the only English pope (Hadrian IV), may have been Vicar of Binsey.

The pub is the Perch which will be remembered by old hands for its decrepit charm, but that disappeared in the fire which gutted the place in 1977. Rebuilt decently enough with a laboured air of tasteful authenticity (flagstones, beams, thatch) which is the sign of true brewers' blight. A large child-proof garden behind, from which a narrow path through a copse leads to the river.

The cutting down of 'a fresh and fallowing folded rank' of poplars is mourned by Gerard Manley Hopkins in his poem 'Binsey Poplars felled 1879'.

nsey, Wytham Hill behind

BLACKFRIARS
5B

Dominican Priory. The dingy front on St Giles' (Eric Gill inscription ove the entrance gate) masks a large barn-like chapel unadorned except fe Stations of the Cross. Clear glass in five-light windows, only the ea window unscreened by surrounding buildings. A gloomy place even on sunny day.

BLACKWELL'S
6C

The relentless demands of higher learning and of mass tourism have bee coolly assimilated by Blackwell's. The immensity of the book-stock are the efficiency of the service are disconcerting and admirable but some e the inexpressible values of bookselling have been lost in the worldly ethe of a management operation. But a visit is something to be undergone. The kingdom has been decentralized in recent years with separate shops for at books, music and records, paperbacks, children's books, and antiquaria books. You will find what you want no doubt, with satisfaction but no much pleasure.

BLUE BOAR STREET
7C

Much enlivened by Powell and Moya's new quad for Christ Church whie backs on to it.

Woods and lanes and large houses in large gardens make it the most agreeable of Oxford's suburbs and the least accessible.

Sir Thomas Bodley (1545–1613, knighted 1604) was a Fellow of Merton who, as ambitious academics were wont to do, abandoned University life for the royal service (he was Queen Elizabeth's ambassador to the Netherlands, 1589–96) and on his retirement in 1598 came back to Oxford with a rich wife, to seek an outlet for his energetic talents. 'I concluded', he said, 'at the last to set up my staffe at the Librarie-dore in Oxon; being throwghly perswaded that, in my solitude and surcease from the commonwealth-affayers, I coulde not busie myselfe to better purpose than by redusing that place (which then in every part laye ruined and wast) to the publique use of studients.'

The University library in 1598 was much as it had been when Bodley had entered Magdalen College as an undergraduate nearly forty years before — 'a great desolate room', the books all gone and the library furniture sold off, the victim of the impoverished economy of the University.

That is a description of the room built above the Divinity School to house the library at its second foundation by Humfrey, Duke of Gloucester in 1489, and still called 'Duke Humfrey' after him. Little in it has changed since Bodley's day. The iron chains have gone – in 1769, 19 hundredweights (965 kilograms) of them were sold for scrap – but a paradise for scholars it remains (although A. E. Housman once referred to it as 'that arsenal of divine vengeance', which is perhaps how it appears from Cambridge). Already within a generation of Bodley's death it was a paradise amplified to accommodate the relentless flow of books, which came – by purchase, by gift, and especially by the terms of the agreement negotiated in 1610 between Bodley and the Stationers' Company whereby the Stationers undertook to send the Bodleian Library a free copy of every new book they published – to augment a book-stock that grew (as it has always grown: today it stands at over 4 million volumes filling more than 110 kilometres (70 miles) of shelving) more rapidly than provision could be made for it. In succession Arts End (1612), the Schools Quadrangle (1613–19, originally partly, later wholly, for Library use), and Selden End (1634–7) were built and the 'Old Library', as it is called, was complete.

It stands to the north of the Radcliffe Camera, a three-storeyed quadrangle, almost square, with windows, battlements, and crocketted pinnacles, disciplined in an almost martial fashion. The plain dignity of the exterior translates into a composition of unrelieved severity inside the quadrangle: the four tiers of narrow blind panelling of the west (entrance) front, the heavily moulded horizontals of the string courses, and the uniform squared windows, with the paved yard between, are together decidedly uncheerful. Even the five-storey tower on the east, designed to illustrate the Five Orders of Architecture (from bottom to top, Tuscan, Doric, Ionic, Corinthian – framing a statue of James I, in a coarse modern copy, offering his published works to the University and to Fame – and

Composite), loses its decorative possibilities in the summary formality of its conception – reminiscent of the elaborate engraved title-pages found in books of Bodley's own time.

For relief the eye must turn elsewhere. To the bronze statue of William Herbert, 3rd Earl of Pembroke (Chancellor of the University, 1617–30), with its touch of Stuart swagger: although he did not fight in any war he is depicted in full armour. To the great window above the entrance doorway, with its curious tracery – for all the world like an art nouveau candelabrum. To the friendly doorways of the old University Schools from which the quadrangle takes its name, with their old names stylishly painted in gold on blue.

Access to the Library is through the Proscholium, the airy vaulted vestibule to the Divinity School, with its permanent exhibition of the Bodleian's finest books and manuscripts. A modest staircase in the north-west corner leads to the galleried Arts End, full of polished oak and oiled calf, and the splendours of Duke Humfrey – especially the brilliantly coloured panelled ceiling, each panel painted with the arms of the University with Bodley's arms on intervening bosses.

A modern extension, the New Bodleian, lies to the north on the corner of Broad Street and Parks Road.

BONN SQUARE
6B

Named (1976) for Oxford's German sister city and, perhaps appropriately, is the spot where the aggressive commercialism of the new Westgate development begins to assert itself. New Road Baptist Church (founded 1653) maintains a classical and reticent presence.

BOTANIC GARDEN
7D

In 1621 Henry Danvers, Earl of Danby, leased from Magdalen College 5 acres (2 hectares) of meadow outside the city walls which until their ejection from England in 1290 had been the Jews' cemetery; he raised the level of the ground and enriched it with 4,000 loads of 'mucke and dunge', enclosed 3 acres (1.2 hectares) of it within a wall 450 metres (500 yds) long and 4 metres (14 ft) high, and by 1633, when Nicholas Stone had completed his grand ceremonial gateway, Danby's Physic Garden – since he had specified a garden for medical purposes, i.e. a herbarium – had assumed its recognizable modern form.

It is a wonderfully refreshing place in a city where nearly all space has confining and perceptible limits, and it grows increasingly peaceful as one moves away from the High Street. Two walled enclosures, the first laid out with formal beds, the second much more romantic – massed borders in the English fashion, exuberant bowers of roses, chock-a-block with trees, at the furthest turn of the path a dark pool and a majestic stone urn. It is a place for assignations, a place where one is likely to frighten a rabbit round a sudden corner, a place for the serious minded (for it is a museum as well as a garden) and for the serious loafer intent on killing a summer's afternoon.

Beyond the walled enclosures, along the banks of the Cherwell below Magdalen Bridge, is a range of glasshouses full of exotics. The first

35

conservatories were built in 1670 – they were heated in sharp weather by hauling round the pathway
an iron wagon filled with burning charcoal – and they have been renewed seven times, most recently i
1968–70. They now number nine and include houses for ferns, water-lilies, orchids and bromeliads
palms, and the New World Gothic of cacti and succulents.

Between the Garden Buildings and the High Street is a rose garden. It commemorates the research i
Oxford which established the clinical importance of penicillin and was the occasion of an unforgivab
act of vandalism and one that has not been forgotten in Oxford: the felling in 1953 of a magnificen
stand of *Sequoiadendron giganteum* (Sierra Redwoods or Wellingtonia), the noblest and longest lived c
all trees, to make way for it.

BRASENOSE COLLEGE
6C

There are not many two-faced colleges in Oxford – All Souls, Balliol, New College in a spaced-out way – and none as admirably two-faced a Brasenose. The entrance façade to Radcliffe Square has a lot to compet with and sensibly doesn't compete too strenuously: a gate-tower of goo proportions followed (towards St Mary the Virgin) by the library and th east end of the chapel, with three nice oriels, one high up on the tower.

The other face is the long decorative range on the High Street; seve bays with gables and a gate-tower in the middle, each bay with a richl treated oriel and another oriel at the corner. It is a genuinely friendly well-intentioned building which sets out to please and succeeds i pleasing. Now for the surprise: it is by T. G. Jackson (1886–9, 1907–9) It is Jackson in his Hertford period; there he is sympathetic, here the moo is accommodating for he obviously looked at the Radcliffe front an decided to follow it. Not meekly of course for that isn't Jackson's style: th vigorous orielization is his signature.

The Old Quad entered from Radcliffe Square dates from the founding c the college in 1509. It has a continuous range of close-set dormers broke only by the hall on the south side, which run out at the same height as th ridge of the roof into which they are set; prominent therefore and giving strong rhythm to a quadrangle in which the fenestration is otherwise fair random. The hall on the south is a modest room with panelling of 1684 an a tunnel-vaulted plaster ceiling of 1754; the original Brazen Nose is fixed the panelling beneath a Stuart coat of arms. A large statue various described as 'Cain and Abel' and 'Samson killing a Philistine with th jaw-bone of an ass' stood in the middle of the quadrangle from 1727 to 188 and was by all accounts a very arresting piece. It is a regrettable loss in a cit habitually over-cautious in its statuary.

The Chapel Quad is a much more surprising place. A cloister, not muc more than an enclosed passage way, runs across the front of the librar along the top a frieze of carved swags divided into bays by flat column each bay with a pair of glazed oval windows like twin portholes; at the f end a doorway with a dainty double arch. Not at all gimmicky but neither it what Oxford cloisters prepare one for. It is of 1657–9 and not obvious representative of Cromwellian virtues.

Nor is the chapel which was being built at the same time, 1656–66. did well to get built at all during the Commonwealth in the university Archbishop Laud. As though in response to the confused political curren of the time it hangs suspended between two worlds – windows trying to Gothic, classical urns as well as medieval crockets, and, most extraordina of all, inside the roof is fan vaulting. But it is a fan vault in plaster, painte and applied over a fifteenth-century hammerbeam timber roof remov from the chapel of St Mary's College of Augustinian Canons (now Frew Hall), put up here in 1656, and covered with the new vault some yea later, but the hammerbeams, pendants, and wall posts of the wooden ro are left projecting below the plaster. There is in the antechapel a memori tablet to Walter Pater, Fellow 1864–94. In it he is flanked by portr medallions of Plato, Dante, Leonardo da Vinci, and Michelangelo. That is audacious too.

New Quad beyond is Jackson's High Street front on the inside and it is just as satisfying looking in on itself as looking out at the world. Behind it, squeezed into a back yard is a landmark building in post-war Oxford: Powell and Moya's infill of 1959–61. If it had only discovered for colleges the possibilities of impossible sites it would have earned all the praise that has been heaped on it. But it did a greater thing: it liberated Oxford into an idiom that within twenty years produced St Catherine's and Wolfson and Wadham library and that takes it beyond gratitude.

BRASENOSE LANE
6C

A medieval laneway with a medieval gutter. Connects the Turl and Radcliffe Square. In the Second World War popularly known and enjoyed as Fornication Lane, presumably because the darkest place in blacked-out Oxford. Now given over to parked Suzukis, Hondas, and Yamahas and college kitchen smells.

BROAD STREET
6C

It can't quite make up its mind whether it belongs to commerce or to learning and the resulting compromise is very effective. The north side breaks refreshingly at Trinity College which is like an English country house to Balliol's manse-like *gravitas*, and further on Blackwell's adds colour and life to the monumental cluster at the Holywell end. On the south side the stretch between Turl Street and the Cornmarket is a variegated and satisfying refinement of the commercial energy of the Cornmarket of which it is an extension. Opposite Balliol a cross inset in the road marks the spot where Latimer and Ridley met their death at the stake in 1555, and Cranmer was burned in 1556.

BROAD WALK
7C

Constructed out of the debris from two centuries of building at Christ Church, it was laid out in the seventeenth century by John Fell, Dean of Christ Church, who also planted the great avenue of elms which by the early nineteenth century were much depleted, by 1900 had been reduced to 'a few battered fragments', finally destroyed in the Dutch elm epidemic of 1975–8, and now all cut down.

BULWARKS LANE
6B

Skirting the Oxford Canal basin on the site of which Nuffield College stands, it follows the line of the Norman ditch, part of the defensive works of Oxford Castle.

CAMPION HALL
7C

An old house (the ancient Micklem Hall), a big garden, the front along Brewer Street with a chapel on the top floor and a garden range, by Sir Edwin Lutyens (1936), constitutes the Oxford house of the Society of Jesus.

CARFAX
6C

Oxford's crossroads – *quatre voies* according to one plausible etymology – and from the earliest times its geographical centre. It was in a tavern near

here that the most famous episode in the University's history began, wh
in 1355 a group of scholars, including two beneficed clergy, came 'to t
tavern called Swyndolnestock, and there took a quart of wine and thr
the said wine in the face of John Croidon, taverner, and then with the sa
quart pot beat the said John without reason'. That was on the feast of
Scholastica (10 February) and the riot which erupted between scholars a
townsmen raged for three days, leaving sixty-three students dead in
wake.

Carfax tower was originally the tower of the city church of St Mar
(demolished 1896). There are views from the top but they are mu
inferior to those offered from the lantern of the Sheldonian.

CASTLE	In 1071 Robert d'Oilly, the first Norman sheriff, built a castle on t
6B	familiar Norman plan: motte or mound, and bailey surrounded by a ditc

The castle mound is prominent and visible opposite Nuffield College;
trace remains of the stone keep (displacing earlier Anglo-Saxon hous
excavation has revealed) which stood on the top of it. D'Oilly also found
St George's chapel built against the outer wall of the bailey to the south
the motte; of this the crypt remains and the west tower (early twelf
century) which doubled as a defensive wall-tower. The outer limits of t
ditch can still be followed in the line of Bulwarks Lane, Castle Street, a
Paradise Street. It was this ditch that the Empress Matilda, daughter
Henry I, widow of the Emperor of Germany, crossed in the winter of 114
after a three-month siege by King Stephen whose throne she claimed: '
night she was let down from the tower by ropes and escaped. She fled aw
and went on foot to Wallingford.'

The tower and curtain-wall now fall within the bounds of Oxford Pris
– Victorian, Dickensian, and glum.

CASTLE STREET	In Anglo-Saxon times probably the main route out of Oxford to the we
7B	crossing the original 'ox ford' at North – or Ferry – Hinksey. Its long

and its importance are clear from excavations which have revealed eighte
levels of road surface, the lowest seven dating from before the year 11
The modern road follows a different route, the result of realignment
Norman times when the castle was built, and again in the last ten years
the Westgate development.

CATTE STREET	In the Middle Ages the centre of the Oxford book trade but now, in its w
6C	the most dignified street in Oxford. It has no commercial establishme

and only a single private house, the Principal's Lodgings at Hertf
College.

CHERWELL	The Thames (Isis) has only a passing interest in Oxford, the Cherwel

Oxford's own and worthy of the place. A resolutely pastoral river, ab
Parson's Pleasure it runs through open meadows and fields; below it has
intimate and meditative air, tree-hung and full of private places. Best s

from a punt, but walks skirt it as it meanders through the University Parks, past St Catherine's, Magdalen, the Botanic Garden, and Christ Church Meadow.

CHERWELL BOATHOUSE
1D

A crisp, gabled and tiled building well set on a pastoral stretch of the river just below Wolfson College, with access from Chadlington Road. The nicest spot to take a punt from in Oxford.

CHRIST CHURCH
7C

Christ Church has always been provoking rather than provocative – full of colour and full of contradictions, proud and overbearing, erratic and unpredictable; in short, all of a piece with the character of its Founder, Thomas Wolsey. 'A man undoubtedly born to honour, rather some Prince's Bastard than a Butcher's son, exceeding wise, fair-spoken, high-minded, full of revenge, vicious of his body, lofty to his enemies were they never so big, to those that accepted and sought his friendship wonderful courteous, a ripe schoolman, thrall to affections, brought abed with flattery, insatiable to get, and princelike in bestowing, as appeareth by his two Colleges at Ipswich and Oxford.'

That is a near-contemporary view, and if he appears larger than life, well, Thomas Wolsey – Archbishop of York, Cardinal of the Roman Catholic Church, Chancellor and in effect Prime Minister of England – was. Once he had asked for and (in April 1524) got a papal bull authorizing the suppression of the Augustinian Priory of St Frideswide at Oxford he acted against twenty other monastic houses – deprecatingly described by him as 'certain exile and small monasteries' in which 'neither God was served, nor religion kept' – in the space of twenty months, and their revenues were transferred to his new foundation of Cardinal College.

Wolsey's master, Henry VIII, who approved of Wolsey's plans, by 1529 had ceased to approve of Wolsey, and after Wolsey's fall the new college was itself threatened with dissolution. But in 1532 Henry VIII refounded it and in 1546 confirmed his refoundation when he established it as the cathedral church of the new diocese of Oxford, by name the Cathedral Church of Christ, traditionally Christ Church, by habit 'the House'.

In its buildings Christ Church has always taken trouble to live up to its exalted beginnings: 'so well and sumptuously built that it might be a royal castle' (1710); 'strikes every eye with its magnificence' (1820); 'majestic' (1963); 'this tremendous college' (1965); 'princely' (1978). And it is indeed uncommonly large – it has, as Pevsner points out, the largest Oxford quadrangle, the largest single eighteenth-century building, and the largest Gothic Revival range. It makes no concessions to timidity and is architecturally the most self-assured college in the University.

It also has a premeditated air. It offers nothing in the way of surprises to match Mansfield library, or Worcester chapel, Jackson's stair tower at Hertford, the new library at Wadham, or St Mary's Quad at Oriel – all of which strike the senses with sudden shocks of pleasure and delight. It is all greatly conceived and finely executed, elegantly composed and urbane, and it commands our unreserved admiration; but it fails to engage us in an enlivening way and in the end it is profoundly undisturbing and we take refuge in the easy hyperbole the guide-books prepare us for.

By 1529 when Wolsey took his enforced retirement from public life the south side of the main quadrangle including the hall, part of the east side, and all the St Aldate's front except half of the north range was finished. The St Aldate's façade dominates the street, and following the fall of the land it increases in size as it goes towards the river. Protruding bays with towers and bay windows at the north and south ends, and the immense central gateway with Wren's distinctive but inelegant tower (1681–2), give the range a more powerful 'body' than any other college front.

In contrast, the great quadrangle inside – Tom Quad, called after the bell housed in Wren's tower – is disappointing. It is too big in relation to the architectural interest it provides; the cloisters intended by Wolsey would have helped by reducing the size and giving depth to the surrounds, but in their absence the handsome profile of Wolsey's hall and the massive squat tower next to it (which dates only from 1876–9, added by Bodley and Garner) and the Fell Tower (in the north-east corner, also by Bodley and Garner, 1876–8) have too much to do.

The hall is approached by an immense draughty staircase which suits but does not match the vast spread of fan vaulting above. The vaulting is not Gothic but Gothic Revival c.1640; the staircase is by the versatile James Wyatt (1805) and in its baronial width and stage-like landings it is just what the space requires, but it is neither Gothic nor Gothic Revival. The hall lies through an antechamber many colleges would be glad to have as a hall, with Chantrey's statue of the autocratic and reforming Dean Jackson looking not a bit like a man who made a habit of refusing all preferment (Offered a bishopric, he redirected the offer to his brother with the remark 'Try Bill, he'll take it'.) It is overstuffed with hammerbeams and portraits but the scale is so vast that there is no trouble in carrying it off. The entrance is flanked by portraits of the Revd C. L. Dodgson (alias Lewis Carroll, author of *Alice in Wonderland*) and John Wesley, which shows a sense of humour. Just beyond Dodgson's a portrait of a greater Christ Church man: W. H. Auden. But it is Auden emulsified with no hint of the familiar autochthonic countenance.

The chapel (and Christ Church chapel is also Oxford's cathedral) opens off the cramped cloister, a remnant of the original priory of St Frideswide as is the cathedral itself. The existing building dates from c.1200 but its most prominent feature is the elaborate vault in the choir which is c.1500. It is probably by William Orchard, the man responsible for the magnificent roof in the Divinity School (he is buried in the cathedral) and it is easy to be persuaded of this. It is something of an architectural juggling trick and the way Orchard in its narrow span achieves the marriage of the complicated vault bristling with ribs, bosses, and pendants, with the multiple tiers of arches and windows is so brilliantly carried off that it disguises the fact that it is not really successful. For the rest, the cathedral is bewildering in the profusion of its architectural detail and the variety of its decoration and monuments. Yet it never loses its chapel feeling; and collegiate it steadfastly remains as any examination of the monuments will show.

Non-collegiate and therefore pre-Reformation monuments include a very sorry-looking piece – the shrine of St Frideswide, heavily restored in 1889–91. It is surprising that there was much left to restore considering the disturbed history of the saint's remains. By 1289 (which is probably the date of the original bits of the existing shrine) she had already been resited at least twice. In 1553 it was thought convenient to bury with her a German ex-nun nicknamed 'Fustyluggs' whose hobby was carving plum-stones into curious faces, and whose misfortune it was to be the first woman ever to reside in an Oxford college. She was the wife of Peter Martyr, the favourite Protestant theologian of Edward VI and a canon of Christ Church; hence in 1557 the indiscriminate counter-reforming zeal of Queen Mary's reign led to her exhumation, and her bones were buried in the Dean of Christ Church's dunghill. Later, on the accession of Elizabeth, they were restored to the shrine, but 'so coupled and mixed' were saint and usurper that they were sealed up together with the ironic epitaph 'Hic jacet religio et superstitione'.

That stands in the north choir aisle, just north of the altar. Further north again and directly opposite it stands a two-storeyed chapel, the lower part stone the upper wood, both with ceilings and elaborately pinnacled. It is a watching loft from which the shrine of the saint could be guarded.

Also opening off the cloister is the Chapter House, a much simpler and peaceful place with a lovely pure thirteenth-century window and everything else to match. It contains a permanent display of the college silver and of Lewis Carroll memorabilia, and a life-size cartoon for the main lights of Burne-Jones's east window in the south choir aisle of the cathedral (1876), installed in memory of Edith Liddell, Alice in Wonderland's sister in real life, whose death was chronicled with such gloomy relish by Dodgson in his diary.

Blocking everything on the south is the Meadow Building (1862–6), a Queen Mary of a range which on the inside has no Christ Church Meadow to relieve it.

North and east of Tom Quad, Peckwater Quad (1705–14) with the library (1717–72) and beyond that Canterbury Quad (1773–83), by Henry Aldrich, Dean of Christ Church, Dr George Clarke, Fellow of All Souls, and James Wyatt, respectively. Surprisingly, the two earlier and amateur architects upstage the professional. Aldrich's Peckwater displays a more fastidious and rigorous classicism than Wyatt ever achieved in Oxford; the library is more monumental than anything Wyatt ever attempted, massive in its proportions and elements.

The design for the library called for the ground floor to be left open, but it was enclosed to accommodate the rich bequest of paintings and drawings which came to Christ Church in 1765 on the death of General John Guise. Although great names are much more common in Guise's collection than great works there are some especially fine examples of Italian primitive and old master drawings. Two hundred years later the college decided to house them as they deserve and Powell and Moya's picture gallery (1964–7) lies beyond the south range of Canterbury Quad. It is a L-shaped concrete bunker half buried in a corner of the Deanery Garden (supposedly the setting of Alice's adventures in Wonderland) with access similar to the 'roads' of open-cast coal drifts. The main galleries open off to the right like a series of monastic cells, with plain rendered walls, stone flooring, and all toplit by natural light and secured by formidable steel gates. Elegant and economical, it could not be better.

CHRIST CHURCH MEADOW 8C	It is not the University Parks but it offers pleasures the Parks do not: easy access from the heart of the city; Oxford's finest architectural skyline – Christ Church, Merton, and Magdalen – taken in at a single sweep; and two rivers, the Cherwell and the Isis in their most animated stretches.
CHURCHILL HOSPITAL	The site of a third- or fourth-century Romano-British pottery industry with visible remains of kilns and drying houses. Examples of the pottery produced here have been found on sites all over southern England.
CLARENDON BUILDING 6C	Hawksmoor, its architect, is on record as favouring the preservation of 'antient durable Publick Buildings' and the Clarendon Building is perhaps a model of what he had in mind. It is hard to imagine a less perishable structure than this with its raised portico of immense Doric columns and its solemn, unyielding windows.

We owe it to the affection for Oxford of Edward Hyde, 1st Earl of Clarendon, Chancellor of the University from 1660 to 1667. In his memory his son made over to the University the copyright of Clarendon's *History of the Rebellion and Civil Wars in England*, written in France after his dismissal from the Chancellorship of England and his subsequent impeachment; it was published in three monumental volumes in 1702–4 and despite the embezzling of most of the proceeds of this and the second edition by the President of St John's enough money was available to start construction in 1711. The University Press moved into it from the Sheldonian Theatre in 1713 (though the imprint *Oxoniae e Theatro Sheldoniano* continued to be used in Oxford books until 1759), and remained there until 1830. The Delegates of the University Press still meet in a fine panelled room on the south though the building is now part of the Bodleian Library.

Statues of the Muses in lead and (in two cases) fibre-glass embellish the roof; a statue of Clarendon stands in a niche on the west side.

CONVOCATION HOUSE 6C	A severe room and, with its dark oak panelling, simple benches, and stone floor, eloquent of gravity and judgement proper to a room which during the Civil War (1642–6) housed the Parliament of England. Beside it the Divinity School, which it opens off, seems almost frivolous, and the absence of electrical lighting in the Convocation House wholly natural.

The middle-aged will remember the Clarendon Hotel with its slightly faded claim 'Under Royal Patronage'; it was demolished to make room for Woolworth's (Lord Holford, 1956–7) and the pattern was set. It could be worse. At street level Babel seethes, for this is Oxford's shopping place – and it has a raw life that the Westgate shopping precinct round the corner lacks. Over the heads of the crowd there is a fair bit to interest the eye but not much to satisfy – a mixture of styles struggling to assert themselves against the relentless homogenization of modern commercial architecture. Distinctive buildings are few – the Golden Cross Inn, fifteenth- to seventeenth-century ranges clustered around a cobbled courtyard; the coarse rubble tower of the Anglo-Saxon church of St Michael-at-the-North-Gate; the late-medieval house at the corner of Ship Street with its overhang and bleached half-timbering; at the Carfax corners Lloyds Bank and the Midland Bank make strong statements in a mannered, extrovert, and unbanklike way.

Shakespeare is said by John Aubrey to have stayed at the Crown Inn (now no. 3 Cornmarket, 14 metres (15 yards) north of High Street on the east side) on his journeys to Warwickshire. In a room known as the Painted Room on the second floor are the best Elizabethan wall-paintings in Oxford (discovered 1927), dated between c.1560 and 1581. There is no reason to believe that Shakespeare ever slept in the room as is sometimes claimed.

Clarendon Building,
Delegates' Room

To the casual visitor Corpus is a bare little quadrangle on the route from Christ Church to Merton. To many Oxonians it is the college they would most prefer to be a member of after their own. Its appeal is hard to pin down. Partly it is a matter of size, the possibilities expressed in the idea of a college as *familia* as well as *communitas*, partly of style – serious, responsible, civilized, unpretentious, urbane, qualities which represent the better self most of us would more often like to be.

Richard Fox (*c*.1448–1528), Founder of Corpus, was a compact of such qualities, as a man who enjoyed the friendship both of Erasmus and Cardinal Wolsey had to be. At the accession of Henry VII (1485) he held in turn the bishoprics of Exeter, Bath and Wells, Durham, and Winchester, preferments designed to support him while engaged in government business as Lord Privy Seal from 1487 to 1516. He worried about his neglect of his spiritual duties, confessing that of his four cathedrals two, Exeter and Wells, he had never visited, besides 'innumerable souls whereof I never see the bodies'. In 1517, retired from royal service, he founded Corpus.

That elusive fit between an institute's life and the willed purpose of its founder is exemplified in the history of Corpus and, appropriately, in the plain sufficiency of its buildings. The only immoderate gesture is the hammerbeam roof of the hall which is a bit heavy handed and elaborate in such a restricted space. The library (1604), as an eighteenth-century traveller remarked, is 'neither large nor unusual', but was praised by Erasmus who said (with affectionate exaggeration) that Corpus's 'Trilinguis Bibliotheca' – referring to Fox's emphasis on Greek, Latin, and Hebrew in the regime he prescribed for his college – would attract more students to Oxford than in times gone by had been drawn to Rome. It is on the same plan as Merton – i.e. medieval stall system, with fixed benches which have the ball ornament that at Merton they lack – but only a single room as against Merton's two; and Corpus is less self-consciously charming. The chapel is just as undemonstrative except for the impetuous modern glass in the east window.

Beyond the chapel lies the Fellows Quadrangle, no more than a yard really, a sparse cloister down one side, with a good plaster vault. Fellows Building itself looks away from the college towards Christ Church Meadow, and should be seen from there. An undeniably grand job, it seems more of an outlier of Christ Church than part of Corpus. John Ruskin preferred living in it to anything Christ Church, his own college, could offer when he returned to Oxford in 1870 as first Slade Professor of Fine Art. It was in his rooms here (Staircase 2, first floor right) overlooking the Meadow that he gathered his young men – Alfred Milner the reformer of Empire, Arnold Toynbee the social philosopher, and Oscar Wilde among them – for breakfast before they went out on their road-building exercises at Ferry Hinksey, undertaken so that they could enjoy 'the pleasures of *useful* muscular work'.

Convocation House

The great sundial in the Front Quadrangle was erected in 1581. It is a

reminder that Corpus, by electing to a fellowship in 1517 Nicholas Kratzer, a German mathematician who established in England horology as a science and 'dialling' as an art (as tutor to the sons of Sir Thomas More he had taught them 'all the astronomy he knew'), bears much of the blame for implanting that most self-righteous of English habits, punctuality.

COUNTY HALL
6B

Norman (1841), castellated and turretted in an unconvincing operatic sort of way.

COWLEY

The original communities of Cowley St John, Temple Cowley, and Cowley village still appear on maps, but have been long obliterated by the remorseless spread of the British Motor Corporation factories. Nothing of character remains except the church of St James, Beauchamp Lane, a Norman church which belonged to Osney Abbey and enough has survived a severe Victorian restoration to remind us of that, although the best thing is the east window of the thirteenth century.

COWLEY PLACE
8E

A cul-de-sac surrounded by the back yards of St Hilda's College and Magdalen College School. A nice, square, skewed house (no. 2) makes a case for the picturesque which neither the school nor the college can answer.

DEPARTMENT OF ENGINEERING
4C

This (1960–2) and the new Metallurgy Building to the north have bol(
strayed from the ghetto anonymity of the Science Area and have carriec
off rather well. The two blocks, one slightly lower than the other, hav(
satisfying mixture of forms and textures and from the Parks are a great h(
to an otherwise uninteresting skyline.

DIVINITY SCHOOL
6C

The Divinity School is an undercroft to Duke Humfrey's Library in 1
Bodleian, although it was built before it. Not many things in England c
match the controlled exuberance of its late fifteenth-century vaulted ro
It was added as an afterthought when the building was virtually compl(
and is of the most elaborate design: a dense tracery of ribs centred on pa
of lantern-like pendants, encrusted with sculptured bosses (455 of the
carved with shields of arms, monograms, initials, figures, flowers, a
foliage; some groups of bosses carved with letters, when taken toget)
spell out inscriptions – 'Ihc. (= Jesus) mercy Ladi help', 'Thank G
of al'.

The vault is very low (it hangs over the spectator like a benign thre
and the light through the windows north and south makes for brilli;
clarity of detail. The west end of the School is surrounded by a narr
raised balustraded platform with pulpits facing each other; here candida
(for degrees in theology, since this is the Divinity School) were examine(
oral disputations in the presence of a moderator – a practice which cea
only in the last century with the introduction of written examinations. 1
arrangement gives material expression to the pleasure Oxford has alw
taken in disciplined combativeness. The Gothic doorway on the north v
inserted by Christopher Wren in 1669 to give access to the Sheldon
Theatre on ceremonial occasions. The small door in the west wall op
into the peaceful twilight of the Convocation House.

The Divinity School is during the summer months flooded with touri
it is best seen on a sunny November day when it is free of them. It ;
houses a permanent exhibition of the Bodleian Library's treasures.

DRAGON SCHOOL
2D

An uncoordinated straggle of nondescript buildings surrounding expar
of playing fields on the Cherwell just below the Cherwell Boathouse. M
favoured by academic families and formidably successful in promo(
success.

EXAMINATION SCHOOLS
7D

The architect, T. G. Jackson, wrote that he was inspired by a 'haunt
vision of Elizabethan and Jacobean work' in his design for the Examina(
Schools, and with that he rather surprisingly managed to get the c(
mission against competition from such middle Victorian heavyweight
Bodley, Champneys, and Deane, and the Schools were built 1876–82.

Jackson's model is secular, not ecclesiastical, and more precisely Ki
Hall in Northamptonshire. Light, from the vast Elizabethan wind(
throughout. Spacious, the whole of the top floor of the three-sided qu
rangle given over to two huge rooms (the Schools themselves), and

Opposite: Examination
Schools, main staircase

entrance lobby with its hammerbeam roof, the size of a college hall. Mosaic
flooring; marble pillars; elaborate brass door furniture; and a grand, grand
staircase.

Grand pictures too, since the 'State Portraits' of the University – Royal
Personages, Chancellors, Stewards, etc. – have been housed there since
1910. Not many of them will repay careful examination, but one will: the
portrait of Chichester Samuel Parkinson Fortescue, Lord Carlingford, by a
painter Ruskin thought worthy of his contempt, condemning him as a
painter of 'vulgar society' (by the Goncourts refined to 'that ingenious
exploiter of English idiocy'): James Jacques Joseph Tissot.

EXETER COLLEGE
6C

Exeter is medieval in its origin (1314) but the college has spent much
energy over the centuries in fashionable excesses, and not obviously to its
profit. The Turl Street front has been rebuilt on four separate occasions
the chapel three times. Only part of a fifteenth-century gate-tower, now in
the north-east corner of the Front Quad, survives from the original
buildings.

The entrance quadrangle is a breakneck place, with Sir George Gilbert
Scott's towering chapel on the left and the hall on the right. The trouble is

5

the chapel which, though it was built later than most of the surrounding buildings (1854–60), by its prominence and by its very great height dictates the scale and controls the eye's expectations. It displaced a modest seventeenth-century chapel (it had to be destroyed by gunpowder) because of a need to accommodate the increase in college membership in the middle of the nineteenth century. It is just conceivable that such showiness and elaboration is what the college had in mind.

Scott took for his model the Sainte Chapelle, the Chapel Royal of the Kings of France, in Paris and a very Victorian replication it is. It has none of the Sainte Chapelle's chaste simplicity; it is a restless agglomeration of special effects. The forest of vaulting with its heavy bosses and attendant capitals and corbels; elaborate canopied stalls with heraldic shields; tiled chancel with marble trim; mosaic and gold-leaf reredos framed in claustrophobic arches; decorative stone gallery with gilded organ; the stained glass, bright but without brilliance. It leaves one gasping for air.

William Morris's tapestry, *The Adoration of the Magi*, to a design by Burne-Jones (both Exeter men), is submerged by the accumulation of detail and deserves a more peaceful setting.

The Fellows Garden offers Exeter's only escape from the intrusive presence of Scott's chapel. It lies to the east of the hall and transplants a woodland glade into the heart of the University. In summer it filters the strong south light which floods the Divinity School and Convocation House which abut on the north, and it also provides the only commutation of the Bodleian's austere public face. Scott was also responsible for the college library which lies beneath the walls of the Bodleian; of the same date as the chapel (1856), it has an altogether lighter touch.

FOLLY BRIDGE
8C

A stout early nineteenth-century bridge over the Thames at a place popularly believed to be the site of the original 'ox ford', but not so: that was at Ferry Hinksey.

Before it was Folly Bridge it was Grand Pont, named after the giant medieval causeway which spanned the marshes between Hinksey Hill and St Aldate's, in which it was a central link. At an early date a gatehouse was built on it and that somehow got entangled with the memory of Roger Bacon, the thirteenth-century Oxford Franciscan and scientist. It was believed that he astrologized from it, hence the gatehouse came to be known as Friar Bacon's Study and came to be regarded with superstitious wonder.

Bacon's 'folly' was pulled down in 1779. In 1849 another was built, and the bridge is worth crossing to see it: no. 5 Abingdon Road, Isis House, in the nineteenth century called 'Caudwell's Castle' after the eccentric who built it. It is a Frankenstein of a building, a loony Victorian Gothick fantasy – fake rustication around doors and windows in red brick, brick battlements and canopied iron balconies, Gothic niches with stone and iron statues, wrought iron applied with abandon everywhere. It is a remarkable thing. What did Ruskin make of it?

FRIARS' ENTRY
6B
Gave access in the Middle Ages to the Carmelite priory in the general area of Gloucester Green, now to the Bus Station from Magdalen Street and the city centre beyond.

GEORGE STREET
6B
A lively shopping street with one of T. G. Jackson's early buildings lying in wait half-way down it, recently cleaned and now quite startling. It was built (1880–1) as the City of Oxford High School for Boys – T. E. Lawrence was a pupil there – later the College of Further Education, now the Social Studies Faculty Centre. Opposite the New Theatre, the George Café (gone), a fashionable Oxford meeting-place of the twenties and thirties, was the only restaurant in England with punkahs.

*; 'Caudwell's Castle', a
*teenth-century folly, Isis
*se, Abingdon Road

*t: The Grapes, George
*t

55

GLOUCESTER GREEN
6B

The present Bus Station and car-park (with Beaumont Street to the nort
are on the site of Beaumont Palace, built by Henry I for his own use – h
son Richard I, 'the Lion-Heart', was born there – which later passed to th
Carmelite Friars. Nothing remains except fragments in a garden i
Woodstock Road (no. 300) and perhaps some pieces in the yard of a hou
on the north side of Beaumont Street (no. 28). Subsequently a market pla
until the coming of the omnibus.

The handsome Bus Waiting Room (1900–1) was originally a schoo
house, and is built to the size of the cottages which formerly surrounded i
pretty bay windows and a strong roof, above the door a carved relief
King Alfred addressing schoolchildren.

GODSTOW

The Thames becomes the Isis here for a few kilometres and has done sinc
the fourteenth century. Much visited because of the Trout Inn, a sham
less tourist trap with trout, ducks, a rustic bridge, and a dishevelle
garden; it now lies in the shadow of a bypass and somehow deserves i
Across the river sparse remains of a Benedictine nunnery (founded 1133
the burial place of Fair Rosamond, mistress of Henry II, and said to hav
been murdered by his queen. Her remains were much venerated by th
nuns.

GOLDEN CROSS INN
6C

Something special in Oxford – a pub of real architectural interest. S
around a deep cobbled courtyard with public rooms opening off, it h
excellent domestic work of the fifteenth and seventeenth centuries. Th
outside with gables, oriels, timbered façades, and, in season, windov
boxes, makes a picturesque composition. The inside is standard Brewer
Eclectic and unworthy.

GREEN COLLEGE
4B

A gift of £1 million from Dr and Mrs Cecil Green of Dallas, Texa
transformed what was to have been Radcliffe College into Green Colleg
designed to serve the needs of medical students and teachers in th
University. The Radcliffe Observatory and its ancillary buildings wi
when adapted for collegiate purposes, form the centre-piece of the ne
group. At present (1979) only the lodge range, sturdy, triple arched, ai
classical, and a cobbled yard beyond, are completed.

GREYFRIARS

A leviathan of a building and unattractive in a coarse-grained way with i
jarring mixture of grey flint and red tiles. The Friary is a Permane
Private Hall of the University (i.e. it is licensed to admit undergradua
but does not have full collegiate status). The adjoining church of :
Edmund and Frideswide has a spruce white-painted interior with a ve
unecclesiastical collection of wrought iron in the chancel.

HALIFAX HOUSE
5D

The University Graduate Centre for those who do not have or who do n
wish to have a college affiliation.

HEADINGTON QUARRY The source of the notoriously soft Headington stone long used by Oxford colleges for their buildings, and longer regretted as it slowly crumbled away, until in most cases it was expensively replaced in the restorations of the years after 1956.

HERTFORD COLLEGE The history of Hertford represents the triumph of hope over experience; it
6C is a college with a continuous existence since the thirteenth century (only Merton and Balliol are certainly older) which did not enter on a settled and secure career until 1874. In the course of 500 years it was sold by a community of nuns who did not own it, and fought off long-standing and vigorously pressed claims of the Fellows of Exeter College that it belonged

Hertford College

to them; it survived the reduction of its corporate body to a single Fellow (who was half mad) and no undergraduates, and the collapse of part of its buildings 'in a cloud of dust'; as a final indignity it was investigated by a commission which concluded that it did not exist, was made over to the University by Royal Letters Patent, and then transferred, lock, stock, and barrel to another Oxford Hall which had lost its buildings in a fire.

Hart Hall, as it was originally called, was one of the innumerable small residential halls of the medieval University and seems to have been established by Elias Hertford not later than 1283. It became Hertford College in 1740. In 1818 it was supplanted by Magdalen Hall. In 1874 it was refounded as Hertford College with the help of a generous benefaction from Thomas Baring, the Victorian banker.

Its complicated history is reflected in the agreeable disorder of its architecture. From Hart Hall remains (all in the entrance quadrangle) the hall itself in the left-hand (north-east) corner, Elizabethan; the whole of the range opposite the lodge – early seventeenth century to the left, a four-bay eighteenth-century house to the right; and the old chapel of 1716, now the library, in the south range. From the period of Hart Hall, but coming into the possession of the college only in 1898, is the octagonal Gothic Chapel of Our Lady, on the corner of Catte Street and New College Lane, dating from about 1520 and thus the oldest part of the college buildings. Magdalen Hall is represented by the two plain buildings (1818–22) at the ends (north and south) of the entrance front on Catte Street – described in a Victorian guide-book as 'painfully like private hotels'. That to the south is the Principal's Lodgings.

The new Hertford of 1874 celebrated its independence by choosing T. G. Jackson, that most independent of Oxford architects, for its rebuilding programme; the rest of the college is largely Jackson's work. If his 'Bridge of Sighs' (1913–14) across New College Lane is the most spectacular part, the most satisfying is his central façade opposite the Bodleian Library (1887–9): two generous bay windows framing triple Venetian windows over the lodge archway, a vigorous balustrade along the roof line with decorative urns on projecting pedestals. It is more restrained than one would expect from Jackson in full cry – see his Examination Schools of ten years earlier – but finely judged for this site.

Behind this the main quadrangle and Jackson, with fine judgement again, left most of the bits and pieces inherited from Hart Hall, but the rest is his. Most striking is the gorgeous corkscrew tower with big round headed windows which follow the planes of the circular staircase it contains. This leads up to the hall, behind Venetian windows, subdued and kitchens (not at all subdued, as summer readers in the Bodleian well know), but worth visiting for the pleasure of climbing the Alice-in-Wonderland staircase. To the north Jackson (1895), and more Venetian windows. Jackson's too the chapel (1908) in the south-east corner; it is on a cramped site and his rich mixture of Renaissance motifs and unattributable Jacksonianisms need more space than it offers to make their case. Only S

Mary's Quadrangle at Oriel is as strong-minded and uncompromising in it eclecticism as this, and that is monumental in a way that the Hertford quad, despite Jackson, is not.

Jackson also did over the North Quadrangle across New College Lane Beyond that, opening off Holywell Street, is a new quadrangle (1976 fashioned out of a corner between Holywell and Bath Place. It is a nice jol which unites five old houses with large sash windows on the Holywell from with a group of new buildings in buff brick, very keen to make a virtue o plainness. A one-storey extension contains a lecture room and commor room. Matter of fact, daring, and successful in a laconic way.

John Donne, the seventeenth-century 'Metaphysical' poet, was member of Hart Hall; the late Evelyn Waugh was to his chagrin a membe of Hertford. Dr Richard Newton, an eighteenth-century Principal deserves to be remembered for his principles at a time when Oxford wa not a very rigorous place: he introduced statutes ordering the life of th college, so elaborate that they prescribed the way meat should be carved and served, the way in which lectures were to be given and work corrected the hours undergraduates were to work and when they were to be allowed to receive visitors. Tutors were to supervise eight undergraduates, adjacent to whom they were to live. Not more than eight men were to be admitted each year, and the tutor was to be responsible for their education through out their time at the University. The Principal, if he 'delight in th education of youth', and 'it shall be made worth his while', might have on pupil himself. Newton's regime was the wonder of Oxford; it was looked on very favourably by parents.

HIGH STREET
6C

The High Street runs from Carfax to Magdalen Bridge – chiefly commer cial towards Carfax, the rest belongs to the University. Its pre-eminence a a streetscape is unchallenged and it cannot be analysed. It must be seen an it is best seen walking briskly from Carfax towards Magdalen; for it is th total experience that counts, and delight evaporates if separate bits ar taken singly and at all solemnly.

HOLYWELL FORD
6E

A good stone house on the site of Holywell Mill, it lies at the dead end o Mill Lane, and is built on an arm of the Cherwell which runs rathe muddily through the grounds of Magdalen College, and is used as Fellow's house by the college. In 1945–6 while the house was occupied b the historian A. J. P. Taylor, Dylan Thomas, then in a highly emotiona state, reputedly camped out in the garden for nearly a year.

HOLYWELL MANOR
5D

Balliol College annexe next door to St Cross church, the gabled Mano Road range together with the church forms a nice rustic, though hardly manorial, grouping. Much rebuilt and only bits of the sixteenth-centur building remain. The unkempt little Gothick quadrangle to the south contained by a dilapidated wall on the St Cross boundary, is the ruin of Victorian chapel.

HOLYWELL MUSIC ROOM
6D

A sonata in a city which goes in for more or less unfinished symphonies. A cool, spacious room, articulated by sweeping balustrades which contain the central doorwell around which rises a single tier of shallowly raked seats. It is a place made for the intimate urbanities of the sort of music that is played there. The chandeliers were used in Westminster Hall for the Coronation of George IV, who presented them to Wadham College, which owns the Music Room. It was built 1742–8 for musical performances, the first public concert hall in England.

HOLYWELL STREET
6D

It cannot altogether escape the overpowering Victorian insensitivity of the New College street front but traffic has been diverted in recent years, and restored to pedestrians and bicyclists it is now possible to enjoy the street as it deserves. From Catte Street to Mansfield Road on the south and Mansfield Road to Longwall on the north is especially good and is best taken at a sweep from the New College side of the Mansfield Road junction. To the right, as far as the eye reaches, seventeenth- and eighteenth-century houses amiably jostling each other, none individually distinguished yet no discordant detail either, whether twentieth-century door furniture or Victorian chimney-pots. Cool inviting interiors. Pastel but not too pretty. It is all very enviable.

HYTHE BRIDGE STREET
6A

Off-loading point for Oxford's water-borne traffic from the earliest times until the closing of the canal basin in this century. The sinister glass and concrete building at the lower (west) end is Blackwell's. It handles their overseas book trade and is of a size commensurate with the business conducted from it.

IFFLEY

An undulating stone-built village on the Thames only 3 kilometres (2 miles) from Carfax and it is not easy to see how it has managed to escape suburbanization. But it has always been a remote place: in the thirteenth century a recluse by the name of Annora lived there.

Iffley Church is a first-rate example of a Norman village church and one which has found its way into the textbooks. But confronted by it one needs to be an archaeologist before enthusiasm can displace dutiful respect. There is no better site for the study of geometrical Romanesque carving – zigzag, beakhead, and sawtooth – and it is most lavishly applied and deeply cut. The west front is thick with it (and on the principle that it is impossible to have too much of a good thing, the rose window was added by a Victorian restorer) and so are the vaults and arches inside. The fine south doorway offers lively relief with figures and animals carved on the capitals.

INDIAN INSTITUTE
6C

A building of character, as they say, and one that does a lot to enliven an important site overshadowed by the expressionless monumentality of the Clarendon Building on the one hand and the New Bodleian on the other. Basil Champneys was the architect and his success lies in his instinctive understanding of what the commission required – an instinct which also

served him well but took him in quite a different direction in his wo
on Mansfield College. The Indian Institute (1883–96) and Mansfie
(1887–9) were being built at the same time less than 800 metres (hal
mile) apart, and in Manchester the John Rylands Library was also going t
to his design; Champneys must have enjoyed commuting between them

The difficulties of the peninsula site he overcame in the most forthrig
way, by planting a tower – and a nice full-bodied thing it is – right on t
corner and running his façades, firmly organized but different from ea
other, away from it along Catte Street and Holywell Street. The tower is
three plain curved stages decorated with two bands of playful carving, o
of mixed oriental and classical motifs, the other portrait medallions
shallow relief of a tiger, elephant, bull, and lion; it is crowned by a cupo
crowned in its turn by an elegant gilt weather-vane of an elephant witl
howdah.

The Indian Institute, originally important as a training centre i
students entering the Indian Civil Service, has, with the loss of Empi
lost its purpose, and the building is now occupied by the History Facu
Library. The Institute's excellent library has been removed to a penthot
on the roof of the New Bodleian.

ISIS The name of the River Thames in its Oxford reaches, but in practice its i
is restricted to maps, guide-books, and volumes of nostalgic reminiscenc

JERICHO Oxford's first suburb, a nineteenth-century working-class district betwe
4A the Oxford Canal and Walton Street, largely preserved and historically f
of the University. Now a peaceful backwater enlivened by some sm
pockets of industry and commerce and well stocked with pubs. Thon
Hardy's Jude the Obscure lodged here (in the novel it is called Beershe
and Hardy worked for five years for Arthur Blomfield, the architect o
Barnabas, the parish church of Jericho, which figures in his novel as
Silas.

JESUS COLLEGE Jesus was founded in 1571 by Queen Elizabeth I at the expense of H
6C Price, Treasurer of St David's cathedral, Pembrokeshire, and a butch
son. To celebrate Price's munificence the college possesses not one
three portraits of Elizabeth, two of them probably contemporary. C
which hangs over the high table in the hall, is very fine, showing the Qu
as no doubt she liked to be represented in middle age – sumptuo
dressed and bejewelled, and decorated with strawberries, cherrie
pansy, and a thistle.

The First Quad, entered from Turl Street, is endearing in its unpre
tiousness: hall, chapel, and Principal's Lodgings crowd two sides of
small quadrangle but with just enough diversions in its detail – the
window to the left of the hall, the clock with battlements climbing ove
the shell-hood over the door of the Lodgings, the apologetic pedime
door to the chapel – and in its surprises – the canted walk with as

metrical lawn panels, and the alarming subsidence of the hall range. All this seventeenth-century work with some Victorian restoration.

The Inner Quad is a much tenser place. The continuous courses of moulding taking in both doors and windows in all three storeys, answered by curvilinear gables just as relentless in their rhythm make one long for a bit of impulsive fudging here. In the south-west corner, above, is the Old Library – one of Oxford's small, least-known pleasures; a long plain room with homely bookcases and furniture and a gallery running lengthways down one side. No ostentation, no real comfort, a place for books not readers.

Furthest from Turl Street and in fact filling one side of Ship Street are two long sad-faced ranges (1905–12), less appealing on the inside than the Ship Street front leads us to expect. The college ran its own chemistry laboratory here from 1908 to 1947. Beyond this the Old Members Building of 1969–71, unsettled and unsettling, full of straight lines but desperate in the lengths it goes to avoid right angles. It is a reminder that difficult sites do not always generate resourceful and satisfying solutions as so much recent work in Oxford would lead us to believe.

JOHN RADCLIFFE HOSPITAL   A white-tiled spread on the north flank of Headington Hill which when completed is going to be very large indeed.

KEBLE COLLEGE
4C   John Keble (1792–1866) was a nineteenth-century Oxford saint and after his death no time was lost in memorializing him. The commission went to William Butterfield; the college was built between 1868 and 1882 – it opened in 1870 – and it is Butterfield at his strongest and most fanciful.

Oxford found the architecture not at all to its taste (Ruskin abandoned his daily walk in the Parks because of it), but a hundred years on Keble has an oddly restrained presence considering its bulk and general bravura. From the outside the chapel dominates (not without competition from the Nuclear Physics Laboratory's towering concrete accelerator at the other end of Keble Road), but inside everything is much more balanced. To right and left of the large entrance quadrangle (Liddon), chapel and hall-with-library (divided by a big oriel which marks the head of the monumental staircase) face each other equally enough across a square sunken lawn and Butterfield's characteristic polychrome brickwork (red, yellow, blue – a contemporary writer thought it 'a pity that the architect's fondness for loud and striking colours was not kept more in check') enlivens and lightens the massive walls in an agreeable way.

There is an easy forthrightness here that is characteristic of the rest of the college, most notably in the boldness of the recent extension along Black-hall Road (1973–7, Ahrends, Burton, and Koralek) made possible by generous benefactions from Sir Charles Hayward and M. André de Breyne. It is a powerful curving yellow-brick range, largely windowless to the street but strikingly translates on the inside into four crystalline storeys of smoked glass with a glazed sunken walkway along the base. Bastion-like

Keble College, Hayward Quad

Opposite: Keble College, chapel

at the Museum Road end it subsides towards the north to a much mor
manageable scale, a sensitive accommodation to the site and a concession t
neighbourliness.

Architecturally a dramatic gesture, it represents an aggressive secu
larism which is a well-judged response to its time in a college with
long-standing reputation (not altogether deserved) for hearty Christianit
and High-Church Anglicanism. Such careful defiance is courageous, an
as if to secure its new convictions Keble in 1979 elected its first non-cleric:
Warden.

The chapel deserves all the attention it gets and must be one of the mo:
cheerful places in either Oxford or Cambridge, and the ubiquitous colou

fulness of the decoration (bricks, tile, mosaic, stone, wood, wrought iro
enamel, paint, gilt, coloured glass), quite un-English in its uninhibitedne
and profusion, reconciles all but the most ill-natured reservations in
happy atonement. Butterfield conceived the chapel as in some w;
analogous to the affecting pieties of Keble's *Christian Year*, but I
obviously and fortunately got it wrong.his other thought was to provide
monument to the Oxford Movement and here he was closer although ma;
Tractarians might well have found it a bit too vigorous for comfort.
side-chapel added later, which Butterfield disapproved of, houses Holm;
Hunt's *Light of the World*, a picture which lives up to Carlyle's judgeme
of it (a judgement passed standing in front of the picture and the painter)
'empty make-believe'.

The hall is surprisingly intimate for such a long room (it is longer th
Christ Church hall). One feels it would be a church nave if it could. Mu
elaboration of surfaces, not all of it symmetrical. The gallery in the mid(
of one of the long sides, with arcade beneath, is a curiosity.

The Warden's Lodging in the south-east corner is a dim buildi
looking into a pretty paved courtyard and encircled at ground-floor level
a wrought-iron balcony.

KEMP HALL Better known today as La Sorbonne, it lies down a passage behind I
7C High Street. A timber-framed seventeenth-century house crowding
narrow yard with its shallow oriels, jettied gables, and large lantern on r
chamfered High Street corner. It is as good inside as out.

KING EDWARD Depressed commercial street which even the life of the High, on to whic
STREET opens, cannot infect. Cecil Rhodes had lodgings here while an und
6C graduate at Oriel.

KINGSTON ROAD North extension of Walton Street, full of humble, unimproved nineteen
3A century artisans' houses for the most part. Towards Aristotle Lane, wh
runs off it, the houses on the west side back on to the Oxford Canal.

KYBALD STREET A peaceful cul-de-sac between the High Street and Merton Street, w
7D almshouses, and stopped by a small square – a nicely composed group
gable ends (Grove House), a Gothic archway, and an overhanging pine

LADY MARGARET The earliest women's college (founded 1878), it occupies a large site at
HALL north-east corner of the University Parks. What should be an inviting fr
2D at the head of Norham Gardens presents to the eye a blank red-brick v
with a heavy pedimented entrance gateway, pierced by two rows of b
hearted windows. Behind lies the main (Wolfson) quadrangle, r
Georgian of various dates (anticlockwise from the lodge, 1926, 1£
1909–10, 1957–61) and styles; three storeys (four to the north) is one
many and the quadrangle has a pinched look as a result. More of the s;
to the east, the Deneke Building (1931) quite grand in a laboured way.

Beside all this rather self-conscious Englishry the chapel and the library strike dissonant notes. The chapel, Byzantine, dumpy, octagonal, was designed by Sir Giles Gilbert Scott as part of the dining-hall range (Deneke) which it adjoins. It has a fine Burne-Jones triptych. The library, on the first floor of the north range built to complete Wolfson Quad in 1961, with galleries carried round all four sides of a long narrow central space on white Tuscan pillars, is stylish, though you wouldn't know it from the outside.

LAW LIBRARY
5E

A ceremonial approach up four flights of steps enclosed at different levels
in fact by three libraries – the Institute of Statistics, the English Facult
Library, and the Bodleian Law Library in ascending order. The steps lea
into the heart of the group to a terrace at the highest level. From there th
design can be read as a fastidious interlocking of planes – defined b
strong horizontal window ranges with the complimentary motif of bric
bands (achieved by the simple device of cutting every fourth joint bac
from the surface) – and blank brick cubes, which are the reading rooms. I
is a considerable achievement – a well-judged balance between differen
tiated functions and the varied forms of the design without strain an
without mannerisms, which makes it unusual for its date (1961–4) i
Oxford.

Facing it on the other side of St Cross Road the Balliol–St Anne'
Graduate Residence by the same architects (Sir Leslie Martin and Colin S
J. Wilson) employs the same elements – yellow brick and horizonta
window bands (on the front, which looks across Balliol sports ground)
but with an easy randomness of detail and – in the defiantly modelle
staircase – bounce.

LINACRE COLLEGE
4D

Founded in 1962 as a non-residential college for men and women graduate
it recently removed from the old St Catherine's building next to the Poli
Station in St Aldate's to Cherwell Edge (at the junction of South Par
Road and St Cross Road): a large Queen Anne house with a Gothic chap
by Basil Champneys (1907).

LINCOLN COLLEGE
6C

Lincoln stretches along the Turl between Exeter and the former Cit
Church of All Saints. That description comes easily to the tongue and n
altogether fairly. Though it is unassuming and unassertive Lincoln hold
its own in the shadow of its pushy neighbours.

But it might have been a different story. Lincoln was always a po
college, and like many institutions threatened not so much by its ow
poverty as by the generosity and energy of the rich. Fortunately, th
college had the knack of deterring benefactors. William Smith, Bishop
Lincoln, in the sixteenth century found the college reluctant to accept th
conditions of a proposed gift so he decided to found Brasenose instead. I
John Radcliffe in the eighteenth century actually made provision to enric
Lincoln, of which he was a Fellow, but changed his mind and transferre
his benefaction to University College. Sir Nathaniel Crew, Bishop
Durham, Rector of Lincoln 1668–72, had plans to use his great wealth
rebuild the college but the Fellows offended him and he didn't.

The college which survived this disaffection consisted of a pretty pair
small quadrangles, exactly square, the Front Quad built between th
foundation of the college in 1429 and 1479, the Chapel Quad between 16
and 1631 – hence examples, virtually untouched, of two of Oxford's mo
vigorous periods of collegiate architecture. In its reticent way it stands u

well to the obvious comparisons: friendlier than All Souls, less brusque than Oriel, more domestic than either. In not easily definable ways it shapes one's idea of a residential college and gives substance to the idea of *communitas*.

There are not many rooms in Oxford less intimidating than Lincoln hall – taller than it is long (or so it seems) and not very long, underlit, over-furnished, with a deep gallery and canopied fireplace with more prominence than a fireplace should ever be allowed. (It is by T. G. Jackson of course.) The chapel is much more composed and to fine effect: all of a piece, i.e. seventeenth century, except for the late Gothic windows. Handsome woodwork and decoratively panelled ceiling, and, what is unusual, a complete series of contemporary windows (1629–30), probably by Bernard van Linge. And if their chief appeal is the part they play in this excellent ensemble, well, excellent ensemble it is.

Later building lies to the east and south of the original quadrangles. T. G. Jackson's Grove Building (1880–3), Jackson in carpet-slippers. The library of 1906, near the boundary with All Saints church, was the third library used by the college; the fourth (and presumably last) is All Saints itself, part of the original endowment of the college, which was taken over as a library early in the seventies. With its towering bulk and striking position standing outside the line of the Turl Street front it has a presence which, architecturally at least, Lincoln might not have welcomed. But grandeur can be tamed by distance and the intervening churchyard and Rector's Lodgings – a building that has got nothing to lose – are just enough.

John Wesley was a Fellow of Lincoln for nine reflective years before he set out on his first missionary journey to Georgia in 1735 and here, it is fair to say, Methodism was born. Wesley is celebrated at Lincoln with pride. His portrait hangs in the hall; a bust stands in a niche in the Front Quadrangle, beneath the windows of the rooms above the passage way from the Front to the Chapel Quad which, traditionally, he is held to have occupied; and the college has named a room after him.

LITTLE CLARENDON STREET
4B

Not very long ago a shabby little street, now fallen on soft times. The fashion merchants of early Pop came first in the fifties. They were displaced by Laura Ashley and good taste in the sixties. The central part of the street has been completely rebuilt. The University's contribution – the University Chest and the University Graduate Building on the south side – is admirably firm and discreet. Somerville's on the north, with a retail arcade at street level, is stylish. Only the St Giles' end retains its original genial and atmospheric clutter.

LITTLEGATE STREET
7B

Site of one of the seven gates of the medieval city, first mentioned in 1244. Excavations in 1971 uncovered footings of the west side of the gate and of the thirteenth-century town wall.

69

LITTLEMORE Newman abandoned Oxford in 1842 and withdrew to Littlemore (he hel█ the living with that of St Mary the Virgin, Oxford) and he abandone█ Littlemore in 1845 for the Roman Church. Earlier he had planned t█ establish a monastic community there, and in 1835 built a church (St Mar█ and St Nicholas) of the most uncompromising sort: a plain rectangula█ room with a bellcote. A thirteenth-century font from St Mary's is a relic o█ Newman's incumbency, as is the memorial tablet to his mother (1836)█ After Newman's time the church was added to and some decorative accent█ were introduced, including two windows (of 1887) by William Morris'█ business partnership of Morris, Marshall & Faulkner. North of the churc█ is a row of cottages converted by Newman as a retreat.

LONGWALL STREET The long wall is that of Magdalen Deer Park to the east, but historicall█
6D refers to the medieval town wall which lies behind the buildings on the we█ side. New College's Sacher Building (David Roberts, 1961–2) dominat█ the street. It replaced a decaying jumble of lodging houses and its seve█ authority in combination with the sweep of traffic bypassing the Hig█ Street in both directions reduces what used to be a homely and rath█ picturesque street to a charmless functionalism.

MAGDALEN BRIDGE Built to the design of John Gwynn (who also designed the Covered Marke█
7E in 1772–82, it carries the High Street across the River Cherwell. represents, in conjunction with Magdalen Tower, one of Oxford's mo█ tired visual clichés, which in the manner of clichés does a disservice █ both.

MAGDALEN COLLEGE Anthony Wood, not one to be free with praise, called it 'the most noble an█ rich structure in the learned world', its water walks 'delectable as the ban█
7E of Eurotas, where Apollo himself was wont to walk'. If that sounds a b█ decorative we need to remember what a cramped and overcrowded pla█ seventeenth-century Oxford was. Magdalen's 100 acres (40 hectares) ou█ side the town walls, with its generous buildings and great tower, █ meadows and park and river and streams and open skies, must ha█ seemed like an earthly paradise. Over 300 years later it has, more than a█ other Oxford or Cambridge college, a composed beauty and grace in the █ of buildings and setting that gives it the harmony of art.

Which is a bit decorative in itself. But Magdalen always has excited t█ imagination of otherwise unexcitable men as is clear from some of t█ schemes proposed for its 'improvement'. The Oxford Almanack of 17█ shows Nicholas Hawksmoor's: only the Great Tower and chapel we█ to be left standing; a massive new classical quadrangle was to be bu█ incorporating the New Building and, on the same scale, the approach fro█ Longwall into a palace-like courtyard. In 1801 Humphry Repton plann█ to turn the meadow into a lake and the New Building into a Goth█ quadrangle. About the same time John Nash came up with a grandio█ scheme which would have turned the college into something between t█

Palace of Westminster and the Palace of Versailles.

William of Waynflete (1395?–1486), Bishop of Winchester and Lord Chancellor of England, no doubt abandoned an earlier site inside the city for the fifteenth-century garden suburb outside the East Gate so that he could give full play to his princely ideas of what a college should be. That was in 1458. His buildings went up rapidly, incorporating parts of the old Hospital of St John the Baptist – the chapel of the Hospital absorbed into the High Street front, the hall (late thirteenth century) now the kitchen of the college.

gdalen College kitchens.
ginally the thirteenth-
tury hall of the Hospital of
ohn the Baptist

71

Forty years after work began, Waynflete's college was complete – an extraordinary achievement by medieval standards. Waynflete did not live to see that but before he died enough was built for him to want to show it off: he entertained Edward IV there in 1481 and Richard III in 1483.

Magdalen stands in the middle of the shallow curve of the High Street as it approaches Magdalen Bridge and just as the excitement of the High Street itself is subsiding. Through the lodge is a small quadrangle (St John's Quadrangle) which preserves the original entrance front of the college – the west end of the chapel and the Founder's Tower. St John's Quadrangle is amazingly coherent architecturally, considering the variety of its origins: it reads as follows, anticlockwise: the High Street front, at least partly late thirteenth century; chapel, 1474–80; Founder's Tower, 1485; President's Lodgings, 1886–8; Grammar Hall, 1614 – the remains of the original schoolhouse of Magdalen College School; St Swithun's Tower, 1880–4; and the ceremonial gateway, 1885 – replacing one of Pugin (1844) replacing one of 1629–35; carved figures from the earlier gateways are preserved in a room at the foot of the Great Tower. Not only coherent but really very handsome, and notable for the way in which the quietest accents hold their own; the Grammar Hall can stand comparison with the back side of the *camerae* at Worcester as an example of Oxford Picturesque, and the President's Lodgings are simple and sensible. Think what T. G. Jackson was doing to the President's Lodgings at Trinity in the same years.

The cloisters are handsome too with the fine profile of hall and chapel along the south side, behind them the Great Tower; grand but skewed enough and separate enough not to overpower, though not standing alone as Waynflete had planned it should. Despite the additions to the college buildings in the course of five centuries the life of the college still organizes itself around the cloisters as Waynflete intended – hall, chapel, kitchens, common rooms, and buttery are housed here, and until 1933 so was the library. Magdalen cloisters, from their earliest days ringing with life and the echo of traffic, are sometimes compared unfavourably to the cloister of New College which is a burial ground. You pays your money and you take your choice.

The chapel was heavily restored in 1829–34 (by L. Cottingham) and it is fashionable to assume that this was a bad thing. But it is also commonly believed that what was swept away was the 'original' interior. It was in fact a fifteenth-century Gothic shell refitted in the early seventeenth century with 'classical' woodwork and decoration of the period subsequently modified by James Wyatt (who did much modifying of a similar sort in Oxford) in 1785–91, chiefly by the replacement of the medieval timber roof by an imitation vault in plaster. In a drawing of 1811 it looks a very uneasy mix. Although the extent of Cottingham's restoration is clear enough the details are hard to judge; but his good stone reredos is measurably better than Isaac Fuller's painting of the Last Judgement which had filled the east wall since the Restoration, and so is his stone vault

Magdalen College, cloisters

an improvement on Wyatt's plaster. Wyatt was a dedicated plasterer; he did the hall ceiling too, but this was replaced in 1902 by a copy of the original roof. The hall has excellent fifteenth-century panelling and Jacobean screen and gallery.

Two low tunnels under the north range of the cloisters give no hint of what lies beyond – the fairest *view* in Oxford: the New Building of 1733 (William Townesend) fronted by lawns and at right angles a deep herbaceous border stretching along a sunken arm of the Cherwell which runs through the college grounds; on the left the Grove and Deer Park, replanted at the Restoration and all but destroyed by the Dutch elm disease epidemic of 1975–8; to the right the Paddock encircled by Anthony Wood's delectable water walks, which follow the bank of the Cherwell, and from which the New Building looks like a great country house. It is difficult to understand the eighteenth-century appetite for disfiguring it.

Towards Longwall, St Swithun's Quadrangle (Bodley and Garner, 1880–4): Gothic of course, strong, firmly handled, and with fine detailing. (William Morris liked it.) The quadrangle presents a view of the

Magdalen College, Grammar
Hall and Founder's Tower

President's Lodgings, the Grammar Hall, Founder's Tower, Chapel, and
Great Tower, one piled on another in a very atmospheric way. Beyond
that, Longwall Quad (Sir Giles Gilbert Scott, 1928–30) on the former site
of Magdalen College School of which the New Library at the High Street
end (J. C. Buckler, 1849–51) was the schoolroom and hall.

A new building (1960–1) lies at the far end of Magdalen Bridge along a
branch of the Cherwell; it had the misfortune to be built just before Oxford
colleges nerved themselves to allow modern architects the freedom of their
convictions.

**MAGDALEN
COLLEGE SCHOOL**
7E

Part of William of Waynflete's foundation of Magdalen College (1458) and
Grammar School, as famous in early modern times for its teaching of Latin
as it is for the singing of its choristers in the services of the college chapel
today. Until 1828 the school occupied its original buildings on the site of

7

Magdalen College. In 1851 it moved to the building now used as the College Library, in 1894 the boarding house moved to a site just east of Magdalen Bridge, and in 1928 the rest of the school followed.

The school has never really got over that move as is clear from its architecturally accidental conglomeration of buildings, some prefabricated, which lie scattered to the east of Cowley Place; despite a good bit of modern building, of which only the chapel (1964–6) pretends to stylishness, and only the new laboratory and Music School (1974) pretend to originality, it has a shiftless, impermanent look about it. Lovely playing fields, encircled by the Cherwell, are reached by two pretty white wooden Chinese Chippendale bridges.

MAGDALEN STREET
6C

Belongs to the church of St Mary Magdalen, not to the college, and runs only the length of the church and its graveyard – from the south end of which one of Oxford's eye-catching trees overhangs the junction of Broad Street and Cornmarket.

MAGPIE LANE
7C

Originally (thirteenth century) Grope Lane, euphemistically renamed in the eighteenth century. A narrow laneway closed to traffic, it offers the most restful escape from the High Street at its busiest point, opposite St Mary the Virgin. Houses of the seventeenth and eighteenth centuries, gables, dormers, overhangs, some in pretty pastel stucco. A house at the High Street end has a well-authenticated ghost.

MAISON FRANÇAISE
2C

A cultural outpost of the sort the French take seriously, it brings a touch of Gallic severity to the relaxed purlieus of north Oxford. A simple unpretentious building (1962) behind a handsome laurel hedge which also screens Maillol's *Flore*, a naked lady who seems not quite convinced that she belongs there.

MANCHESTER COLLEGE
5D

Notable for its full complement of Burne-Jones–William Morris glass (1893–8) in the chapel, Manchester is the final home of an itinerant eighteenth-century Dissenting Academy (Unitarian) and it is not a college of the University.

Arlosh Hall added later (1913) is manorial rather than collegiate, built in a good rich stone much more agreeable than the cadaverous Derby stone used in the other buildings. The best view of Wadham's brutal new library block – perhaps the only good view – is from the Chapel Quadrangle. The main quadrangle has a disconcerting audience of busts peering out of attic windows.

MANSFIELD COLLEGE
5D

The removal of this Congregational college from Birmingham to Oxford in 1886 so that it could act as a voice for the Free Churches in a predominantly Anglican university was a purposeful act of evangelical witness which demanded a purposeful architectural response. Basil Champneys got the commission and he did well by Mansfield.

Individually the buildings have great self-assurance, clearly conceived and firmly modelled Gothic with careful and unpernickety detailing. There is no striving after effect and there are no dramatic accents; decorum prevails and it is here (as it is not always) an affirmative thing.

The tall chapel is a most delicately balanced composition in which everything is exactly right. In the nave each window is answered by a pair of arches which stand between two sparely moulded piers rising to the roof. Behind the altar and facing down the chapel in the Congregational manner, two rows of raised wooden stalls, with canopies on the second row acting as a reredos. At the opposite end behind an open screen a rich and simple art noveau tapestry fills the space beneath the west window. Its elegance is complemented by the series of memorials cut in the stone on the west face of the columns of the nave arcade, all in the chastest of lapidary styles.

The library, after an unpromising approach through a dark passage and up a staircase lined with college photographs, is a delight. A long space with steeply pitched roof covered with large and boldly painted panels of rather stiff floral decoration and scrollwork in brilliant colour. The roof is supported by simple wooden posts and a most intricate pattern of arched braces, lateral, longitudinal, vertical, and horizontal – giving the impression not of space divided but of space interlocked. The bookcases rise at the posts through two floors, the upper floor a gallery at barely head height – really no more than an upper deck – with a railed catwalk for access. The bookcases on both sides separate reading alcoves lit by four-light oriel windows. A double row of portraits hangs on the balustrade of the gallery overlooking the central space. An ingenious, imaginative, invigorating, and wholly satisfying achievement.

The hall is a disappointment, much better outside than in.

MARKET
6C

Tucked in between the Cornmarket and Turl Street, High Street, and Market Street, and not as humble as it looks; it was designed (1772) by John Gwynn, who was also responsible for Magdalen Bridge. Full of aisles, good smells, red meat, and sawdust.

MARSTON VILLAGE

With the opening of the Marston Ferry Link Road and bridge Old Marston is now very accessible from the centre of Oxford and has lost some of its remote charm, already eroded by the bypass, as a result. But it still maintains a villagy watercolour quality and a cheerful liveliness not found in its genteel neighbour Old Headington.

The parish church of St Nicholas is much better inside than out, with Norman and later work and good fifteenth- and sixteenth-century woodwork. It is famous for its bell-ringing.

MARTYRS'
MEMORIAL
5C

Modelled on the Waltham Eleanor's Cross – the best preserved of those erected by Edward I to mark the route taken by his wife's funeral procession on its way from Nottinghamshire to London – and built (1841–3) to commemorate the Protestant Martyrs Latimer, Ridley, and Cranmer

Market

burned (1555, 1556) for their political errors and their religious conviction on Broad Street near this spot. Generations of undergraduates have passe judgement on it by crowning it with chamber-pots. For some years dis owned by city and University both, and left in disrepair as a result, it is no safe and seemly again.

**MATHEMATICAL
INSTITUTE**
4C

A plain statement adjacent to Keble's extravagances.

MERTON COLLEGE

7D

'This college, according to the time of its endowment, craves the first place of all colleges in Oxford.' Anthony Wood's view was not universally held in his own day. The claims of University College to have been founded by King Alfred, irresistible in combining the romance of legend and the glamour of royal connections (in which Oxford has always taken an ingenuous pleasure), was widely accepted. But Wood, though a Merton man and therefore partial, was a sound historian and knew that whereof he spoke: the statutes drawn up by the Founder, Walter de Merton, the King's Chancellor and later Bishop of Rochester, in September 1264 (replacing an earlier set which have not survived), and charters of 1266–8 which show the college acquiring property in the parish of St John the Baptist, on the site of which Merton still stands.

In 1274 when Bishop Merton gave his college its third set of statutes, Merton's rivals had not yet received their first. So far as University College and Balliol College (as they subsequently became) had a presence in the University it was a merely enabling one – the thirteenth-century equivalent of a Local Education Authority.

Much remains from the thirteenth century. The earliest building is probably the hall, almost completely Victorianized (1872–4) but worth a look for the thirteenth-century door heavy with tiers of original ironwork, like an elaborate doodle. The chapel replaced the earlier parish church of St John the Baptist and was used as a parish church until the nineteenth century. Yet its proportions are those of a cathedral, although a fragmentary cathedral since only the choir and transepts were built. What prompted such an immense building for a college which in 1280, just before the chapel was begun, seems to have had about forty Fellows living in and twenty-five undergraduates living out?

There can be little doubt that the Founder was moved by a spirit of emulation if not of competition. Merton's statutes make clear that he saw his college as providing a training ground for service in church and state; it was to be a training for 'secular' as distinct from the 'religious' life represented by the great monastic institutions of the time and the statutes show the firmness of his purpose: any Fellow who entered a religious order was to vacate his Fellowship.

And anyone who was moved to embrace the religious life in Oxford in the latter part of the thirteenth century was not short of opportunities. The Blackfriars had been established there since 1221 (the first Dominican house in Britain), the Greyfriars since 1224 (both were large houses with between eighty and ninety members by the end of the century); the Carmelites arrived in 1256, the Austin Friars in 1268, and so on. It seems likely that Bishop Merton, aware of the threatening presence of such powerful orders, set out to provide for his new college a dignity that could stand comparison with theirs. We know that the choir of the Greyfriars church, erected between 1240 and 1250, measured about 30 metres (100 ft) in length, that of the Austin friars about 27 metres (90 ft), that of the Augustinian Priory of St Frideswide 20 (68 ft). Merton's choir built

between 1289 and 1297 measures 31 metres (102 ft); the secular foundation was not to be outdone.

There is no denying that Merton chapel is immensely large and those who think it extravagantly so may be echoing the views of the college in the fifteenth century because after the completion of the transepts, crossing, and tower between c.1330 and 1451 no more was built. Perhaps it would be a more satisfying building if it had been completed. But after initial surprise at the vastness of the interior, we take refuge in details: the early fourteenth-century glass which fills the choir windows, and the fine medieval brass lectern; the rich wall monuments to Sir Thomas Bodley (north transept, 1613) and Sir Henry Savile (south transept, 1622) with grave busts and elaborate allegorical ornament, and Savile's including a picture of the college at that date; the glowing green marble font in the north transept given by Tsar Alexander of Russia in 1816. And incongruously, on the wall behind it, old Anthony Wood's memorial tablet at the very spot where, overtaken in November 1695 by a 'total suppression of urine', he had supervised the digging of his own grave. Yet, after all is said, it is hard to be enthusiastic; for it is a place without a heart.

The only other medieval work is Mob Quad (1304–78), a very humble affair after the chapel, which it is on the way to, and which it is contemporary with. Mob Quad is something of an architectural specimen since it is the earliest complete Oxford quad and set the pattern for the rest. The prominent dormers were added in the early seventeenth century to give extra light to the library which runs the length of the west and south ranges on the first floor. The library, except for the shell, is not medieval, which it is popularly thought to be, but early seventeenth century on the medieval plan. It is on the most intimate scale: narrow reading alcoves with benches between projecting bookcases, separated by a central aisle running the length of the room; medieval tiles in the aisle introduced in 1623; woodwork and plasterwork with Jacobean motifs; some books have been left with their chains. A museum piece, sophisticated in an antiquarian way, beautifully kept and full of atmosphere.

Fellows Quadrangle (1608–10) lies on the other (east) side of the hall. It has an unpleasant, bleached and scrubbed look but from the outside surprisingly cheerful, especially as seen from Merton Fields to the south.

Merton's modern buildings for the most part occupy the site of St Alban Hall annexed by Merton in the nineteenth century and rebuilt by Basil Champneys, 1904–10. It is Champneys in a relaxed and playful mood as he is not seen elsewhere in Oxford – Tudor more or less and heavily orielized. (But the gate to the garden, if it is his, sacrifices grace to elaboration.) Further east still, on Rose Lane facing the Botanic Garden, Rose Lane Buildings (1939–40): Sir Hubert Worthington at his very middling best.

On the south side of St Alban's Quad is the Fellows Garden. In the eighteenth century it was open to the public both day and night and acquired an evil reputation. It is bounded on the south by the medieval

on College, antechapel

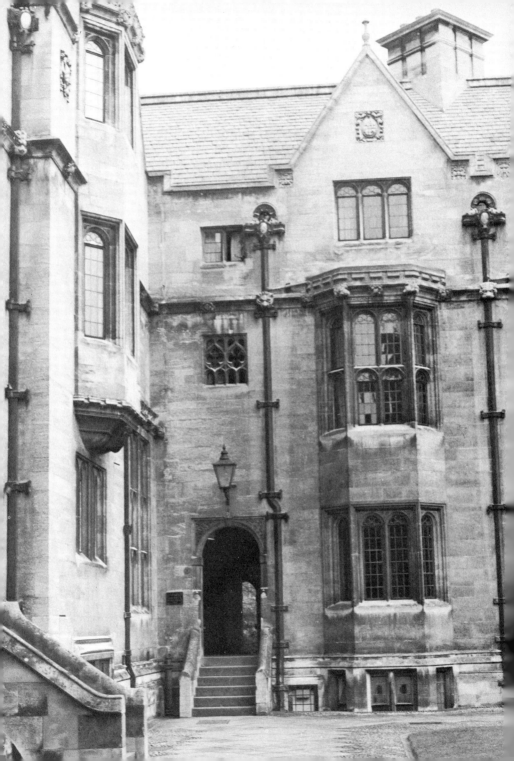

town wall with a terrace walk laid out in 1706, at the north end a very pretty Summer House (1706–7) now used as a music room. It was probably here or hereabouts that William Merle, a Fellow of Merton who died in 1347, for seven years made and recorded the observations that gave him the distinction of being the first person in the West to keep a continuous journal of the weather.

Finally, the Grove Building. In 1864, in an evil hour, says Wells, 'the college cut down their "Grove" and erected their "new buildings" to the S.W. of Mob Quad, from a design of Mr Butterfield; by so doing they spoiled the most beautiful view in Oxford and their own claim to be the most beautiful college in Oxford'. While there is no accounting for taste it is not easy to see what Wells might have been on about or why he worked himself up into such a lather of indignation over it. But the Fellows of Merton seem to have understood: in 1930 poor Butterfield's building was emasculated by having the top storey removed and two wings added. Just such a misguided job as Trinity had done to Wren's Garden Building 130 years before.

MERTON FIELDS
7D

Real agricultural-looking fields lying immediately to the south of the college between the Old Town Wall and Broad Walk.

MERTON STREET
7D

Cobbled and collegiate backwater: Merton, University College, Corpus, Oriel, and Christ Church own and abut most of it. Postmaster's Hall opposite Merton gate-tower is where Anthony Wood, Oxford's great memorialist, was born (1632), lived, and died (1695).

MESOPOTAMIA
5E

'Country between two rivers.' A donnish joke, the name of a stretch of the footpath to Marston on the eastern boundary of the University Parks, where for a short distance it follows a narrow tongue of land lying between the Cherwell and a mill-stream.

MILL LANE
6D

Follows the line of the north wall of Magdalen Deer Park from St Cross Road to Holywell Ford, where the mill formerly stood.

MITRE HOTEL
6C

A famous Oxford inn with a well-documented history from the thirteenth century. The present building dates from the early seventeenth century and has much good architectural detail of the period. For more than 200 years a coaching inn – Anthony Wood (who was a passenger) records 26 April 1669 the first time the 'flying-coach' made the journey between Oxford and London in one day; the fare was 12s. By the early nineteenth century half a dozen coaches a day were leaving the Mitre.

Owned by Lincoln College since 1523, in 1968 the college took over the upper floors for undergraduate rooms. No longer a hotel, the ground floor is leased to a steak-house chain and has lost both its character and its reputation.

MUSEUM OF MODERN ART 7B A converted warehouse in Pembroke Street, it bears lonely witness Oxford to the claims of twentieth-century art.

MUSEUM OF OXFORD 7C An imaginatively laid out civic museum incorporated in the Town H with entrance in Blue Boar Street.

MUSEUM ROAD 5C Tidy terrace houses overlooked by the great south bastion of Kebl Hayward Building and beyond, where it shrinks to a laneway connect with St Giles, the twinned columns framing the recent Sir Thomas Wh building at St John's College hang over the wall like expectant gossips.

NEW COLLEGE
6D

The approach down New College Lane between the blank walls of t
Warden's Barn and the cloister does not prepare us for what is one of t
most sudden and most assertive spaces in Oxford – the Great Quad of Ne
College. Severe castellation (1674) and crisp sash windows (1718) on thr
sides, the hall (1380–6) with its massive buttresses and the Munime
Tower adjoining, rear up on the north; it provides a bracing experience ir
notably unbracing city.

The hall is reached by a steep staircase cut through the lower storeys
the Muniment Tower; it is of great height with wrap-around linen-fo
panelling and dull even as college halls go.

To the east, beyond the medieval town wall (running through the college grounds, here at its most complete, even to its bastions) is a monumental mid-Victorian range of character and not much else. At the west end in the town ditch, the library (1939) lacks even that; its foundations are subsiding and deservedly.

The chapel was, of course, at the heart of William of Wykeham's conception of what a college should be. Built all of a piece with the hall and at one go, between 1380 and 1386, the other principal members (Great Quad, Gate Tower, Bell Tower, Barn, cloister, kitchen) were added in the next twenty years. The idea has survived better than the details of its

embodiment; roof, screen, reredos (for a second time), organ gallery, and most of the stalls, were lost in a confident restoration by Sir George Gilbert Scott (1877–81).

In detail, most of it in the antechapel: fourteenth-century glass by Thomas Glazier with its job lot of apostles, prophets, saints, patriarchs, bishops, etc.; Sir Joshua Reynolds's Nativity with attendant Virtues (1778–85) in the great west window is vapid by comparison. Epstein's *Lazarus*, successful despite its obvious shapeliness, aboriginal and unsanctified. Eric Gill's immense memorial tablet to the New College men who died in the 1914–18 War strikes a different note: folly and waste celebrated in the most unambiguous and elegant way. To the north of the altar Wykeham's pastoral staff is encased and illuminated. There can be few finer European examples of the medieval goldsmith's art.

The cloister adjoining has the depressed air of a memorial precinct which is what it is. The garden at the other (east) end of the college, beyond the Great Quad, is approached through a lovely and elaborate wrought-iron screen (1711). A comfortable rather than a pretty place, with a sunken lawn; a nicely unrefined herbaceous border massed against the city wall which encircles the garden. In the middle a hill – sixteenth century in its origin – with a drunken stairway up it; tree-covered and undergrown with elder, bramble, rosebay willow-herb, and convolvulus, it is a folly to be cherished, bringing just the touch of wilderness that Oxford's obsessive tidiness so seldom finds room for.

**NEW COLLEGE
SCHOOL**
5D

A discreet group of buildings which very much mind their own business and could have had no reason to expect, and no doubt do not much enjoy, the encroachment of twentieth-century brutalism in the shape of Wadham's new library building which stops and just about overwhelms Savile Road.

**NEW INN HALL
STREET**
6B

It may mark the west boundary of the earliest (Anglo-Saxon) town. Frewin Hall, originally St Mary's College, is on the east side, founded in 1435 as a house for Augustinian Canons. Erasmus lodged here when visiting Oxford in 1499; Edward VII, as Prince of Wales, lived here when an undergraduate, 1859–60.

The gatehouse and the entrance range are original. Inside, two eighteenth-century buildings nicely unrestored, and beyond them a new quadrangle (constructed for Brasenose College which owns the site) composed of a row of stone cottages, a new range of six staircases with plain stuccoed façade and simple sash windows, and a rather pompous neo-Georgian brick house – an unlikely but a successful mix.

The building to the right of the gatehouse was the first Methodist Meeting House in Oxford; John Wesley preached there on 14 July 1783 and on several subsequent occasions.

NEW THEATRE
6B

Oxford's only commercial theatre, it now hedges its bets with disco dancing.

NORHAM GARDENS
3C

Much afflicted by parked cars it curves round the north edge of the Parks towards the Cherwell, lined with large and solid Victorian houses, and is stopped at the end by the street front of Lady Margaret Hall. The houses on the south side turn their backs to the road since they were designed to look out over the Parks but with the growth of trees along the boundary they can no longer be seen from there. The University Department of Educational Studies (no. 15) conceals a pretty courtyard behind with a good modern extension; 'Gunfield' (no. 19) adjacent to Lady Margaret Hall has a most romantically neglected garden.

NORTH HINKSEY

Oxford is first mentioned in the Anglo-Saxon Chronicle under the year 912, when it is recorded that Edward, King of the West Saxons, took over London and 'oxna forda', and this 'oxen ford' is now believed to refer to a ford over an arm of the Thames at North (or Ferry) Hinksey, in the low-lying marshland on the western outskirts of modern Oxford. Ferry Hinksey was the scene of John Ruskin's roadmaking experiments in the 1870s.

NORTH OXFORD

A rare example of a Victorian suburb with a continuous history of occupation by the class that built it. It lies between the Woodstock Road and the River Cherwell, extending from the junction of the Woodstock and Banbury Roads in the south to Staverton Road in the north. West it drifts away into lower-middle-class Victorian gentility, north to twentieth-century suburbia. The gardens of the immense red-brick Victorian houses do not trifle with careful edgings of alyssum and lobelia; they burst with mature trees and exuberant shrubberies which in the early summer create a sort of arborial paradise. North-bound traffic grinds away at the crumbling edge of things, but it is still an area to be savoured, on foot on a fine Sunday morning in May.

NORTH PARADE
2B

No doubt it grew up to serve adjacent Park Town when all around was country. Just the right mix – dairy, ironmonger, two pubs, post office – to provide the small commercial disturbance needed to enliven the surrounding red-brick comfort. Round the corner, Gee's greenhouse: a Victorian tradesman's extravagance of the most practical kind.

NUFFIELD COLLEGE
6B

A gift to the University in 1937 from Lord Nuffield and built 1949–60, succeeds in stilling the enthusiasm that is the proper response to its benefactor's munificence. It is a place difficult to praise. The long single quadrangle on two levels affords no opportunities for architectural surprises and in an unforgiving way allows the offences to compound each other. The Cotswold gables are wrong, the crowded rustic dormers are wrong, the stone is wrong. The funereal lodge is like a crypt. And the massive tower which houses the library manages to overpower any residual goodwill. Fortunately, Nuffield is unlikely to corrupt the taste of the young: it houses only postgraduates pursuing research in the social sciences.

Built on the site of the canal basin of the old Oxford Canal Company it is out of the way and, tower apart, unobtrusive, with the special anonymity that traffic-washed buildings enjoy. A Hubert Dalwood fountain in the quadrangle tinkles incongruously. Only the stained glass (by John Piper and Patrick Reyntiens) in the minute chapel disturbs the prevailing listlessness and it is excellent.

OBSERVATORY STREET 3B   Cheerful stuccoed terrace where early nineteenth-century workers' cottages and genteel lower-middle-class Victorian houses outface each other. Belsyre Court at the Woodstock Road end, a preposterous mixture of gables, oriels, balusters, and balconies, around a courtyard, is an early block of flats (1936) which has worn to a kind of apologetic charm. An earlier proposal for the site (1932) offered such amenities as a theatre, a cinema, a dance-hall, and a large car-park, but north Oxford didn't like it.

OLD ASHMOLEAN 6C   Built 1678–83 for Elias Ashmole's collections (see the account of the Ashmolean Museum) it was intended from the first to combine display of Ashmole's natural historical and anthropological artefacts with systematic scientific work. The upper floor was given over to exhibition space, while lecture rooms were provided for the Professors of Natural Philosophy on the ground floor and in the basement – the latter also containing both the first chemistry laboratory in England, and a residence for the Professor of Chemistry. After the removal of the original collections in 1894 the building was used for a variety of purposes – including the editorial offices of *The Oxford English Dictionary*; it is now the Museum of the History of Science.

The Sheldonian is not a helpful neighbour. The last four heads in the series encircling it on the north overlap the Museum's Broad Street front, cutting across the ground-floor windows, spoiling the best view of an urbane façade. Round the corner the massive and ornate ceremonial door faces the west side of the Sheldonian across a narrow yard and its dignity lacks space to assert itself. The stretch of wall beyond, connecting the Museum to the Bodleian north front, was built to display the Arundel marbles (which John Evelyn wanted to protect by planting a hedge of holly in front of them) now in the Ashmolean Museum.

The collections of the Science Museum include clocks and watches, telescopes, microscopes, navigational and surveying instruments, weights and measures, orreries, materials illustrating the history of photography – amongst them a portrait by that well-known practitioner of wet-plate photography, Lewis Carroll – and most notably a magnificent collection of astrolabes, full of cabbalistic beauty.

The most arresting display is of the equipment used early in the Second

World War to develop a technology for the production of penicillin. It i
constructed of an assortment of bedpans and old tins – biscuit tins, coffe
tins (Lyons pure ground), and one labelled 'Agricultural anti stomach an
lung-worm fluid in sheep and lambs'; the control panel (*c*.1940) of th
counter current penicillin extraction apparatus ('As the resevoir bottles c
solvent, crude penicillin, and acid emptied, the relevent lamp on the pan
lit and the bell rang to warn the operator') resembles an over-ambitiou
door bell. It is pure Heath Robinson and very moving. A Pyrex flas
contains one of the original cultures of *Penicillium notatum*, now dried up

OLD HEADINGTON Well-kept antique suburb sitting peacefully between the bustle
Headington High Street and the John Radcliffe Hospital. Some goo
houses of various dates, a couple of farmhouses, and a bright Bapti
chapel; quantities of stone-walling, some cobbled yards, and nice weed
corners. A contented sort of place with the feel of a small country town.

The parish church of St Andrew looks as prosperous as no doubt it is, se
in an enjoyably lumpy churchyard. Norman chancel arch, wide aisle
toy-like font. Fragments of medieval tiles in a case in the chancel. Th
roof is a miscalculation: painted electric blue with red trim, aquamarin
and white.

OLD PALACE Believed to have been the episcopal palace of Robert King, last Abbot
7C Osney and first Bishop of Oxford, 1542–57, later rebuilt. A love
confection of seventeenth-century gables and plasterwork (two especiall
outrageous first-floor ceilings inside), with a double row of delicate orie
on carved brackets. A modern extension down Rose Place (1970–1) is b
contrast very large and very plain in yellow brick.

ORIEL COLLEGE Oriel begins in a rather tight-lipped mood at Merton Street and its thre
7C diminishing quadrangles stacked end to end in a narrow island site gro
increasingly relaxed as they approach the High Street. In no other colleg
do such strongly contrasting styles and textures sit so closely or s
comfortably together. Wadham is comparable but Wadham has mor
space and is, as a result, more loosely organized.

No one would call the Front Quad a genial place and the echo
Wadham is here unmistakable: Wadham was built at a single go, 1610–1.
Oriel's Front Quad dates from 1620–42, replacing medieval buildin
used by the college since its foundation by Adam de Brome, Rector of S
Mary the Virgin, in 1326. The effect here is more fanciful – Jacobea
gables for Wadham's battlements, livelier tracery in the windows of th
eight-window range in hall and chapel and the end bays accentuated b
large oriels. Oriel's central porch with its lumpish statues, no better tha
Wadham's unfortunately, is a much more emphatic affair. But like th
Front Quad at Wadham it is not a spot to linger.

In the middle (Back) quadrangle much is the same but everything
different. The ranges to east and west carry on the style of the Front Qua

Opposite: Oriel College,
St Mary's Quad

Oriel College, St Mary's Quad — although they are a hundred years later (1719, 1729) and there is so⟩
consequent softening of detail reinforced by the nicely disordered so⟩
range which is, of course, the back side of the original scheme of 1620–
for the Front Quad.

But chiefly the lightening of mood is attributable to Wyatt's Pallad
library of 1788. An elegant building of two storeys, and a finely balan⟩
composition it is: rusticated stonework below, smooth above; lo⟩
windows deeply set in round arches, the upper range plain and unscu⟩
tured between single columns; and a heavily moulded parapet over ⟩
Symmetry is maintained too. The library is free standing and of seven b⟩
as were the buildings of 1719 and 1729 until joined to the south range in ⟩
early nineteenth century. And nature comes to the help of art with anot⟩
pair of those inevitable trees: a chestnut and a sycamore stand right and ⟩
of the library – just enough to break the continuity.

St Mary's Quad is another world and another world because anot⟩
college. St Mary's was one of the medieval halls which survived until 1⟩
and hence escaped the single-minded seventeenth- and eighteenth-cent⟩
rebuilding programme of Oriel and the result is delightful.

There is nothing very medieval about the Rhodes Building which glares down from the far end. It is a cyclopean piece even from the back view which it presents to the quadrangle. Rhodes was immensely proud of his Oxford education – in his will he artlessly describes himself as 'Cecil John Rhodes of Oriel College, Oxford' – and he left money (£100,000) to put his mark on the college and did. Built 1908–11, Basil Champneys is the architect, and it displays Champneys's extraordinary knack of realizing in his designs the latent expectations of a commission. Even amidst the distractions of the High Street it is masterful composition; on the inside it presides not so much over the quadrangle as over the college, with a consular authority.

It is a tribute to the sensible strength of the rest of the quadrangle that it can support Rhodes's building and not be outshouted, and it is the variety of its eclecticism that makes accommodation possible. To the south, back to back with Wyatt's library next door, the old chapel and hall of St Mary Hall, now the undergraduate library and Junior Common Room, one above the other – pure Gothic to the eye, with a nice unselfconscious mix of windows – one, two, and three light, variously treated – but in fact of 1639–40. In the south-east corner it meets in a bit of a surprised way a very handsome timber-framed house with strong sash windows and dormers, which seems to have strayed from a country High Street. Opposite, a romantic early nineteenth-century Gothic range with two decorative oriels of the sort Sir Walter Scott must have imagined his heroines sitting in. Everything here calls out the best in everything else and comparison simply reinforces the integrity of the whole composition.

ORIEL SQUARE
7C

Like Bonn Square, it is nothing of the sort, but a space where Bear Lane, King Edward Street, and Oriel Street meet. Named only in 1953 after lobbying by Oriel College which faces on to it. Some nice pastel houses on the north, the monumental Canterbury Gate of Christ Church to the west.

ORIEL STREET
7C

Unperturbed and unrenovated it curves nicely to screen Oriel Square from the High Street. Behind nos. 3–8 is the University 'Real' or 'Royal' (in North American 'Court') Tennis Court, the medieval game from which Lawn Tennis has its descent. Played indoors under cover, it has been an Oxford sport for at least 500 years, four courts recorded as being in use as early as 1508, and later most colleges had their own. Oxford's present one is said to date from 1798.

OSNEY

A quiet backwater of cheap Victorian row housing with industrial infill and an adjacent industrial estate just west of the Railway Station.

It sticks in the memory because of Chaucer's references to it in the 'Miller's Tale'; which would have surprised Chaucer, not only because he was a modest man but because in his day it was famous for a very large and very rich abbey, founded in 1129 as a house for Augustinian Canons, its church more than 90 metres (100 yds) long, with twenty-four altars, and possessing the third-highest tower in England.

At the dissolution of the abbeys the church was chosen by Henry VIII 1 be the cathedral for the new diocese of Oxford but he changed his mind a he was wont to, and in 1546 the seat of the bishopric was transferred 1 the monastic church of St Frideswide (part of the new college of Chris Church) and subsequently the abbey church and buildings were demc lished. All that remains is a small fifteenth-century domestic building (wit a tablet recording the case of a deacon who became a Jew, married a Jewes and was tried and burned for his apostasy) and a short stretch of wall, no part of Osney Mill. The abbey church lay to the east in the preser graveyard, the chapel of which is built within the site of the nave. Oxford most famous bell, Great Tom, migrated from Osney Abbey to Chri Church together with six others – still commemorated in Oxford (an elsewhere) by a pub called the Six Bells.

The modern church of St Frideswide is a sullen-looking building qui untouched by charm or discretion. It possesses a curious Victorian relic: wooden door (displayed just inside the entrance) carved in commemor: tion of the saint, apparently by Alice Liddell, daughter of the nineteent century Dean of Christ Church, and the eponymous heroine of Lew Carroll's *Alice in Wonderland*.

OXFORD CANAL A relic of late eighteenth-century industrial optimism, it was built connect the Thames with Liverpool and the industries of the north via t Coventry Canal and the rivers Trent and Mersey. It now stops dead Hythe Bridge Street just east of the Railway Station. The old canal bas beyond is the site of Nuffield College, and the Canal Company's offic overlooking it provide Lodgings for the Master of St Peter's College. Nor the canal is the boundary of Jericho, edged with mixed commercial ar industrial development, drab Victorian houses, and some energetic urb; renewal. Further north again it runs behind Southmoor Road ar Kingston Road; the tow-path here is crowded with overhanging willows

OXFORD GIRLS' Lusty gardening helps offset the reductive functionalism of the buildin
HIGH SCHOOL Epstein's *Deirdre* is viewable through the glazing of the courtyard.

OXFORD UNION Not to be confused with the Oxford University Students Union, an e
SOCIETY thusiastic undergraduate organization with laudable quasi-political a:
6B reformist aims, which, to the satisfaction of its enemies, it experiences t greatest difficulty in holding fast to for two weeks together.

There is, by contrast, nothing enthusiastic about the Oxford Union. It a University debating society founded in 1823 and ever since a place whe ambitious young men have first tasted the pleasures of public speaking a; political life: Gladstone, Salisbury, Asquith, Harold Macmillan, Edwa Heath, and Jeremy Thorpe all began their political careers here.

The Society buildings form a vaguely collegiate grouping, red brick a uncoordinated, on St Michael's Street, with a convenient back door

Frewin Court off the Cornmarket. The club rooms – dining-room, billiard room, bar, etc. – are dowdy, and overfurnished with cigarette and pinball machines. Only the library, the original debating chamber (1857) designed by Benjamin Woodward and decorated by D. G. Rossetti, Burne-Jones, William Morris, and friends, has any dignity. It is a tall room with a well-used air, tiers of much-scuffed bindings, and cracked leather armchairs around a central marble fireplace. Long, with galleries all round, between the lighting ports of which the Pre-Raphaelite mural of Morte d'Arthur is scarcely visible. The ceiling and arches are brilliantly painted with intricate and crowded foliate decoration by Morris himself.

XFORD UNIVERSITY APPOINTMENTS COMMITTEE
56 Banbury Road
3C

Pevsner calls it 'a yellow brick nightmare castle' and it does look as though it was built for a mad dwarf. In fact it was occupied by Queen Victoria's youngest son, the haemophiliac Prince Leopold, while an undergraduate at Christ Church, 1872–6.

XFORD UNIVERSITY PRESS
4B

A resolute façade (1826–30), classical, with bays and massive Corinthian columns, and an authoritative air proper to a publisher of bibles and dictionaries, and one which has served the learned world since 1478. A stern quadrangle behind, dominated by a very large copper beech with its roots in a raised lily pond.

PARADISE SQUARE
7B

A Victorian slum on the site of a medieval monastic garden (Franciscan) now reverted to waste, a waste of relief roads, bypasses, diversions, and car-parks – all the squalor attendant on fifties' urban renewal and sixties' commercial development. In this intemperate seeking after rational solutions one opportunity was not taken: to redeem the Thames, here a sewage canal, hidden and unnoticed.

PARKER'S
6C

The great bookshop of Victorian Oxford but never managed to reconcile itself to the post-war world; it is now part of the Blackwell empire, left only with the dignity of its name and the largest stock of maps outside of London.

PARKS ROAD
4C

As representative and varied a piece of Oxford streetscape as there is: from Broad Street – the King's Arms, the New Bodleian, and Wadham, followed by a wide tree-lined (limes, planes) walk between the boundary walls of Trinity and St John's on the west, Wadham and Rhodes House on the east, in the middle on the east side a pair of seventeenth-century cottages; then the Institute of Agriculture, Radcliffe Science Library, University Museum, Keble, the University Parks, the Engineering and Metallurgy buildings, with Park Lodge as full stop.

PARK TOWN
2C

A mid-nineteenth-century anticipation of the garden suburb built up the Banbury Road (1853–5) on land originally intended for a workhouse. Two curving terraces of handsome stone houses enclosing a central garden.

Beyond, a raised and weed-fringed terrace of more modest houses screened, no doubt originally for socially cosmetic purposes, by a thicket of trees and shrubs. It has a look that must have made it very stylish when viewed from the dingy medieval clutter of Victorian Oxford – 'An eighteenth-century aftermath/A pseudo – nay, a slipper Bath', as one of Oxford's precisest eyes (Maida Stanier) describes it. Now a bit faded and brackish but struggles to maintain its singular airs and on a good day succeeds.

PARSONS'
PLEASURE
4E

A famous Victorian bathing place for gentlemen who prefer not to wear swimming suits. Hard to find and underpopulated. Near by a weir, bypassed by rollers; to take a punt over them is still one of the adventures of an Oxford summer.

MBROKE COLLEGE
7C

The motives which have inspired the founders of Oxford colleges are various. Piety and its secular post-Reformation equivalent philanthropy – neither always free from the impulse to self-commemoration – account for most. Pembroke is alone in owing its existence to civic ambition.

Thomas Tesdale (1547–1610) was a native of Abingdon and twic mayor of the borough, who made his fortune first as a maltster, later as farmer with a special interest in growing woad for dyeing, and left £5,00 in his will for the support at Oxford of fellows and scholars from Abingdo Grammar School. The Mayor and Corporation of Abingdon, executors c Tesdale's will, decided to make Broadgates Hall, one of the innumerabl residential halls of the medieval University and, in the early seventeent century, perhaps the most flourishing of the survivors – only six college had more members – a college of their own creation instead, and pru dently secured their interests and ensured that their foundation wa 'immovable' by making 'the Earl of Pembroke, then Chancellor of th University, the Godfather of it, and King James the Founder'.

The approach from St Aldate's is messy, with St Aldate's church tc close for comfort and a thoroughly uncoordinated front ending in th squashed gatehouse tower quite unable to hold its own even against suc modest competition. It deserves our attention, however, for Dr Johnsc had rooms on the second floor and beneath it he was habitually see 'lounging at the college gate with a circle of young students round hir whom he was entertaining with wit and keeping from their studies'. Th Old Quadrangle behind, 1626–70 but Victorianized, and in the summ pleasantly over-furnished with overplanted window-boxes, is an anteroo to a much more urbane Chapel Quad.

It is long and just the right shape for the buildings surrounding it; a lar elliptical lawn with broad gravelled walks all round. To the west a hall gigantic proportions which does well what Waterhouse at Balliol attempt and failed to do – marry size and stylishness without exaggeration. It is b J. Hayward, 1848. Adjacent and at right angles another monumen range, also by Hayward but built first (1844–6) and no doubt encourag him to his later boldness in the hall. It is bold because the existing buildin were the back of the Old Quad, facing the hall, with the library at the nor end of the range and chapel to the south, all much more domestic. It rea is a grand working out of a big idea and not at all what such a modest colle might be expected to rise to.

The chapel is a trim classical building of 1732, the interior remodelled 1884 and redecorated in 1972; previously the college had used the sou aisle of St Aldate's. The long south side of the Quad between chapel a hall has a wall with battlements and a row of limes overlooking it from b far side which is the Fellows Garden. 'Garden' is a bit of a joke, a terra rather – and a terrace indeed: it runs along the old town wall which her intact, following the line of Brewer Street. A guide-book of 1820 refers the 'fine view of the adjacent country' which may be got from it.

To the north, as a result of the closing of Beef Lane, a new quadran has been taken in which is bounded by the backs of the houses of Pembre Street; these have been done up very cheerfully and give some sort of he to a group of modern buildings (post-1960) too widely dispersed to ha much coherence. They include two straightforward blocks by Sir Le

Martin, one at the St Ebbe's end incorporating a branch of Barclays Bank.

Francis Jeune (1806–68) was a reforming Master of Pembroke in the middle of the nineteenth century. He commands our gratitude not so much for his reforms as for his very young wife, Margaret, who in her diary recorded her amused skirmishes with the stuffiness of Victorian Oxford. She was a woman of style (she imported her bonnets from France to ensure that she kept ahead of Oxford fashions), spirited (she found the local conventions irksome and boring – 'to use a slang term'), and catty ('Mr Thompson has been elected Provost of Queen's', she writes, 'so little Zoë is become a Headdess').

PEMBROKE STREET
7B

A good mix of seventeenth-century and later houses, not really suspected in the approach from either direction. The only half-stylish fringe to Westgate which abuts the west end.

PITT RIVERS
MUSEUM
4C

John Tradescant's 'Ark of Curiosities' was the original ethnological collection of the University, part of Elias Ashmole's *Antiquarium* opened to the public in 1683. General Augustus Pitt Rivers (1827–1900, a Grenadier Guardsman and archaeologist, who commuted to his excavations in an

open horse-drawn carriage followed by his assistants wearing the General's colours and riding on pennyfarthing bicycles) presented his collection to Oxford in 1883, just as the Ashmolean was developing interests less arcane than might be thought proper for a self-respecting anthropological museum. In 1886 the Ashmolean transferred its ethnological holdings, including Captain Cook's collection of specimens from the Pacific Islands, acquired during his Second Voyage, 1772–5, to the Pitt Rivers.

The original gift of 15,000 artefacts, housed in a gloomy galleried pavilion stuck on to the back of the University Museum and approached through it, has grown to more than a million, and the bewildered visitor may be forgiven for sometimes thinking that most of them are on display. It is the most perfect and satisfying of Victorian relics, a vast anthropological bazaar: Zaïre nail fetishes, Naga head-hunting trophies, mummified crocodiles from Egypt, North American picture writings, Japanese Nō masks, Wanyika friction drums, Haida totem poles, snake-bite charms from Guyana, prey-god fetishes of the hunt from Zūni, River Boyne hide and wicker currachs, snuff-taking appliances from Nigeria, teeth encrusted with lime and betel from betel chewing in Nicobar, membranophonic instruments, fire-making sticks, votive concubine figures, bowls for offerings to ancestral ghosts, hand-looms for weaving horse-hair cloth (there is no compelling reason why this desperate catalogue should stop; best let it subside with the notice occasionally to be seen amidst the museum's overcrowded displays: 'This case is not intended to illustrate anything except our lack of space').

As a universal archive of art, technology, and superstition it leaves nothing to be desired and is not to be missed.

THE PLAIN
7E

A carousel centred on a quaintly housed Victorian water-fountain on the former site of St Clement's churchyard at the east end of Magdalen Bridge.

LANTATION ROAD
3B

A pretty watercolour street of minuscule houses with exuberant cottage gardens. Crowded and a bit claustrophobic, the desperate search for architectural solutions to frankly unpromising sites has resulted in a number of one-off renovations and most are both imaginative and successful, especially in the eastern half. It has infected adjacent development in Leckford Place and St Bernard's Road and the whole area has a toy-town quality that is very appealing.

PLAYHOUSE
6B

The University Theatre, name elegantly carved in stone by Eric Gill.

PORT MEADOW

Oxford's ancient civic treasure, an immense area of open pasture on the east bank of the Thames stretching from the Railway Station to Godstow Bridge far to the north. Horses, cows, and sheep graze it, with the amiable connivance of the Freemen of the city who are its corporate owners. Walks along to tow-path to Binsey and Godstow past a nice clutter of boatyards filled with pleasure craft and long-boats.

103

PUSEY HOUSE
5B

Founded in 1884 as a memorial to Edward Bouverie Pusey (1800–82)
High Churchman, friend of Keble and Newman, and incorporating h
library. The St Giles' front and the small quadrangle behind have a hea
Victorian air (but really 1911–14 and 1921–6): solid dispirited Gothi
The chapel is a surprise and a pleasure. A strong nave of good proportion
late Decorated in style, firmly handled and sensibly lit, it is stopped by
stone screen through which a small door admits to the choir and a ve
theatrical display. A baldacchino with columns and canopy, figures of th
resurrected Christ and angels, foliage, all in gilt and blue, framing a marb
altar with bronze frontal and elaborate candlesticks. Italianate but witho
the careless and liberating Italian vulgarity. It is by Sir Ninian Comper a
dates from 1937. A narrow wall-passage has a cheerful little museum
late-classical (third- to fifth-century) inscriptions, sarchophagi, relie
and other antique bric-à-brac.

**QUEEN ELIZABETH
HOUSE**
4C

Houses the Institute of Commonwealth Studies in a large stone l
seventeenth-century house (Black Hall), with a pleasing modern additi
towards Blackhall Road.

Most founders of Oxford colleges have been bishops, knights, or – more recently – millionaires. Robert de Eglesfield, a native of remotest West Cumberland, was merely chaplain to Queen Philippa, wife of Edward III, and presumably it was for pragmatic reasons that in founding his college in 1340 he called it after his mistress. Ever since royal ladies have kept Queen's in mind: Philippa herself was probably responsible for Edward III's endowment of the college with a rich property in Southampton; Queen Elizabeth formally authorized the use of the name 'Queen's'; Henrietta Maria (Charles I), Caroline (George II), and Charlotte (George III) are all benefactors. And by ancient custom on the accession of a new Queen Consort the Provost of Queen's presents a petition to Her Majesty praying her to undertake the office of Patroness of the college.

In the eighteenth century, although not royal and perhaps no lady (Richard Steele, the essayist, said 'To love her is a liberal education'), the most munificent of its benefactors was Lady Elizabeth Hastings who left her estates in Yorkshire to Queen's to provide exhibitions for North-country children. She was an independent-minded woman and prescribed a novel form of election to the scholarships: the names of the candidates were to be put in an 'urn or vase' and those drawn out were declared elected. The purpose of this was that it 'left something to Providence'; it was last employed in 1859 when the Provost's servant's hat did duty for a 'vase'.

Eglesfield himself does not appear to have put much trust in Providence. His statutes elaborate a code of discipline which any Victorian school-master might have approved of. Undergraduates were to be 'examined' by

one of the Fellows every night before they were allowed to dine; a night-watchman was provided for, whose duty it was to 'whistle at the usual times in the night, that the student might know when it was better to sleep and when to work'; all musical instruments were forbidden except at times of common recreation; heads were to be regularly washed and for this purpose one of the college servants was to be a barber; the Fellows were allowed to possess neither bows and arrows nor dogs. In addition, the Provost and the twelve Fellows were intended to correspond to Christ and the Apostles; their arrangement at dinner was to be the traditional arrangement of the Last Supper; their gowns were to be red to keep them in mind of the blood of the crucified Lord; and they were to be summoned to dinner by trumpet (as they still are).

Time, however, brought some amelioration of this regime. Thomas Crosfield, Fellow of Queen's, on 17 March 1630 recorded in his diary that a Fellow reprimanded for laxness in his chapel duties 'threatened to stiletto Mr Provost', and the next day Crosfield reports 'Some tumultuous coursing betwixt Wadham College and our house'.

Of Eglesfield's buildings nothing remains. Rebuilding began in 1672 and was completed by about 1760 – between, that is, Wren's Sheldonian (1669) and the north range at Worcester (1753–9). There is no denying that the façade, just in the elbow of High Street, makes a very grand and a

105

very classical statement, and neighbouring All Souls and University College look very humble beside it. But most colleges would be glad to put distance between themselves and Queen's. For a comparable combination of a singular architectural idiom and deliberateness of execution on this scale, Oxford had to wait for Arne Jacobsen's St Catherine's in our own generation. Yet we do not know who was responsible for it. Whoever he was his conviction shows.

The Front Quadrangle was built last, presumably because it was here that the buildings of the old college lay: west range 1709–11, hall and chapel 1714, front and gatehouse 1734, east range 1735–60. It is all of unmitigated severity. The hall (to the left) and chapel (to the right) are equally daunting: symmetrical arrangements of massive columns and large windows on either side of a central tunnel. The interior of the hall would be a suitable setting for a last supper, presided over, as the Founder intended, by the Provost seated on the throne which stands behind high table. The chapel is apsidal with a stupendous wooden screen furnished with two more thrones; it has much muddy glass.

In the North Quadrangle the relentless single-mindedness of the Front Quad falters, chiefly because the west range is detached and mildly decorative. The upper floor is the library of 1692–5, with an interior worthy of Wren or Hawksmoor but so far as we know not by either. Oxford does not have anything to equal it nor much to approach it. Its proportions, woodwork, and plasterwork are of such quality that reading there must be pure sybaritism. It is understandable but regrettable that visitors are so firmly discouraged.

Beyond the library a friendly lane gives access to Little Drawda Quad put together from a group of solid houses on the High Street, cottagy and romantic, with a rose garden and suitably decorative planting. Eighteenth-century classicism is here faded indeed. It is known as the Nuns' Garden because traditionally the place where the nuns of St Frideswide's found sanctuary at the dissolution of their convent at the Reformation. To the north, in the Provost's Garden, the former brewhouse; as late as 1939 Queen's brewed its own ale.

QUEEN'S LANE
6D

Car free bends its way between college walls past St Peter-in-the-East, Queen's library, the new Provost's Lodgings (1958–9) at Queen's, Hawksmoor's towers at All Souls, New College gate-tower (where it becomes New College Lane), Edmund Halley's house, and beneath T. G. Jackson's 'Bridge of Sighs' at Hertford; connects the High and Broad Street, and there is no better approach to either.

QUEEN STREET
6B

The extension of the High Street beyond Carfax and now, except for buses, pedestrian only, leading to the Westgate Shopping Centre.

ADCLIFFE CAMERA
6C

Pevsner calls it 'England's most accomplished domed building' and in addition it can lay claim to being one of the most independent. It presides over the pedestrian bustle of its own square in a grande dame-ish way, quite unperturbed by the proximity of some of the most inhibiting presences in Oxford – Hawksmoor's towers at All Souls, Sir Thomas Bodley's Library, and the University Church. The architect was James Gibbs and it was built (1737–49) as a library building (which it still is) with money left for the purpose by Dr John Radcliffe, physician to Queen Anne. Two floors, the upper one very fine – lofty, galleried, with stone-carving and plasterwork; it is reached by a spiral staircase that allows readers to approach their work with dignity.

RADCLIFFE INFIRMARY
4B

Another of Dr Radcliffe's benefactions, built by his Trustees, 1759–70. The original façade is handsome enough but heavily overlain by successive nineteenth- and twentieth-century additions which run away behind into seedy confusion.

The chapel in the forecourt (1864) was the gift of Thomas Combe, Superintendent of the Clarendon Press, designed by Arthur Blomfield, and a preliminary to Combe's subsequent and more ambitious benefaction of St Barnabas. The fountain is a copy of Bernini's famous Triton fountain in the Piazza Barberini in Rome – moss encrusted, with a surreptitious grandeur, a tribute to benign neglect.

RADCLIFFE OBSERVATORY
4B

It remains unscathed by the squalor of the Radcliffe Infirmary yards in which it stands, surrounded by car-parks and prefabricated buildings. Set in fields as it was originally it must have been magnificent; it still has dignity and authority and both will be enhanced when, as is planned, it is incorporated in the new Green College.

It is very early Greek revival (begun 1772) and it is surprising that with such a splendid testimonial as this the style never really caught on in Oxford: Pevsner calls it architecturally the finest observatory in Europe. Henry Keene drew up plans but died in 1776 and James Wyatt took over as he did at Worcester and rethought the design. It was Wyatt's idea to model the tower proper (i.e. the third storey) on the Tower of the Winds at Athens; the Winds are represented in the animated reliefs which are carved in the panels just below roof level. The best view and the best place to enjoy it is from the walled garden on the north side.

RADCLIFFE SCIENCE LIBRARY
5C

Two wings built by architectural knights, both fashionable in Oxford in their time: Sir T. G. Jackson and Sir Hubert Worthington. Worthington's building on Parks Road (1933–4) in his usual roughed-up stone has an uneasy and undulating, typically weak, façade. It screens Jackson's original building of 1901 on South Parks Road, a long range with buttresses and an assertive Venetian window which in its forcefulness raises expectations unfortunately not fulfilled in the buildings of the Science Area beyond.

RADCLIFFE SQUARE
6C

It has no real identity apart from the monumental buildings that surround and define it – All Souls, St Mary the Virgin, Brasenose, the Bodleian, and especially the Radcliffe Camera, which is, so to speak, its sufficient cause. Cobbled and pedestrian but not long cleared of traffic and parked cars, it gives to Oxford the peaceful centre it has long wanted.

RAILWAY STATION
5A

The smelly Victorian slum has been replaced (1972) by one notably less easy to use and much less pleasing to look at.

RANDOLPH HOTEL
5C

If Oxford had a grand hotel this would be it. It is High Victorian Gothic at its most excitable, prompted perhaps by the measured dignity of the Ashmolean Museum opposite. That dates from 1845 and it is easy to be persuaded that twenty years later the architect of the Randolph (William Wilkinson, 1864) was cocking a snook at it.

Tall and more or less symmetrical on its corner site (though extended to the west in 1952), the façade can barely contain the exuberance of the fenestration: long and square headed at street level, followed by three rows (Middle Pointed) set closely in pairs and organized by forceful oriels with roofs, running through three floors; in the roof dormers, at one point in a doubled tier. It is all a bit overwhelming.

Inside life is more peaceful. Edwardian lounge full of polished mahogany, plump buttoned velvet, and gilt. Autumnal dining-room. Handsome open staircase with mirrors framed in pointed arches. Osbert Lancaster's set of large paintings (12) illustrating Max Beerbohm's Oxford romance *Zuleika Dobson* hangs in the public rooms, and they are not at all elegiac.

REGENT'S PARK COLLEGE
5B

Baptist and theological. A single, long, narrow, peaceful, architecturally dull, quadrangle behind a blank façade to Pusey Street.

REWLEY ABBEY
6A

A stretch of low rubble wall and a single fifteenth-century doorway sandwiched between the coal-yards and the Oxford Canal, marking the boundary of a car-park, are all that remain of the house founded by Edmund, Earl of Cornwall, as a 'studium' for members of the Cistercian order. It became an abbey in 1281 and was dissolved in 1536.

RHODES HOUSE
5C

Built in 1929 it is a boring because an unpeopled place, a mausoleum to the imperial ideals of Cecil Rhodes, but insulated by false principles of decorum from the raw energy of those who have come for eighty years to enrich Oxford in his name. Sir Herbert Baker, the architect, must bear much of the blame; he aimed at a harmony between Oxford's classical traditions and native Cotswold craftsmanship and achieved instead a genteel parochialism. (It is exemplified by two 'no-smoking' signs in the public areas: one is in English, hand carved in stone, the other in Greek which translates 'Let No Smoke-Bearing Person Enter'.)

A rotunda crowned with a Zimbabwe bird and with a rather trumped-up

portico is entered from the street. It is a memorial to the Rhodes Scholars who died in two World Wars – including Adam von Trott zu Solz, the German Rhodes Scholar hanged with piano wire by the Nazis for his part in the 'Generals' plot to assassinate Hitler in 1944. Behind, a thirty-room Cotteswolde Manor House overlooking lawns and good borders – a reminder that the site was originally part of the gardens of Wadham. The great hall has an immense oriel window, a gallery, an apsidal east end, and unfortunate chandeliers like defeated spiders.

ROGER BACON LANE
7B

A severe little lane cobbled (1976) out of the ruins of St Ebbe's on the backside of the Westgate Shopping Centre, taking in a manicured garden, a small green oasis in a commercial wilderness, and belonging, appropriately enough, to the offices of the Oxford Preservation Trust.

ROSENTHAL'S
6C

Oxford's most august, esoteric, and unapproachable bookseller.

ROSE PLACE
7B

Begins excitedly with the Old Palace at St Aldate's but goes flat beyond.

RUSKIN COLLEGE
5B

Founded in 1899 by Walter Vrooman, an American, to allow British working men to enjoy the benefits of higher education, Ruskin has had a great and beneficial influence on English society in the twentieth century through its links with the Workers' Educational Association and the administrative ranks of the Trade Union movement.

ST ALDATE
7C

Norman in origin but drastically restored in the nineteenth century when the room over the south aisle, the library of Broadgates Hall before it became Pembroke College, was also taken down. The aisle itself was used by Pembroke as its chapel until 1732. The original Decorated east window has been reset, very handsomely, over the arch between south aisle and south chapel; just below it is a fourteenth-century bone hole.

ST ALDATE'S
7C

In its upper reaches the Town Hall and Christ Church; going south wholesale urban redevelopment as it falls away towards the River Thames at Folly Bridge. Half-way down on the right (west) side is the Old Palace, and further down on the corner of St Aldate's and Speedwell Street excavations have revealed pieces of Saxon Oxford which can be dated AD 780–830, the earliest archaeological remains yet found, and perhaps to be connected with the monastic house traditionally held to have been established by St Frideswide in the vicinity of Christ Church in the year 727.

Number 83 St Aldate's is the little seventeenth-century building said to be the original of the Old Sheep Shop in Lewis Carroll's *Through the Looking Glass*, and trades on it.

ST ALOYSIUS
4B

Ornate Jesuit church hiding behind an unbalanced façade with oversize rose window, just where the Woodstock Road leaves St Giles'. Designed by Joseph Aloysius Hansom (built 1873–5), the inventor of the Hansom cab;

Gerard Manley Hopkins was curate in 1878; the Holy Water stoop is a memorial to him. Interesting in an impure way, it is apsidal with an elaborate reredos consisting of a double tier of saints, portrait heads in roundels above with six round-headed windows superimposed and a pointed and segmented ceiling over all. Richly cut Stations of the Cross set in shallow aisles. A well-stocked Relics Chapel on the north side: relics of St Francis of Assisi, St Theodore, St Felix, and – since this is Oxford – many letters of saints.

ST ANDREW
1C

Big, Norman (1907).

ST ANNE'S
COLLEGE
3B

St Anne's started life as the Society of Oxford Home Students in 1879, founded to look after the interests of non-collegiate women under-graduates. As might be expected, it developed residential ambitions, getting its first building in 1938, but not much else until the 1960s. The late start allowed the college to avoid the deadly emptiness of Oxford architecture between the wars; how lucky it was a glance at the original buildings of 1938 and 1948–51 – Sir Giles Gilbert Scott's last gasp – makes clear.

Shortage of money (no doubt) and a restricted though ample site have encouraged sensible rather than showy or ingenious solutions. The dining-hall (1960) stands next the Woodstock Road; tall and airy with glass on two sides and a circular lantern above. The kitchens behind stretch north to

St Anne's College, Rayne Building

south along the road, to the north of them is a simple tile-hung village house, and north again the Founder's Tower (1966), with oriels and turrets in pre-cast concrete and entrance gateway beneath – something of a sport, a clever bending of old forms to a modern idiom, and incidentally providing the most amiable approach to any Oxford college.

On the further, Banbury Road, side of the campus (here, as nowhere else in Oxford, it seems the right word) are two four-storey residence blocks (Wolfson and Rayne, 1969), concrete again and façades with an assertive pattern of oriels like those of the entrance tower. They are the middle pair of a proposed set of six identical blocks in a flattened S-configuration running parallel to the Banbury Road, and the only two built; to the east they are carried on coved pedestals designed to allow a lake, part of the original plan (also not built), to be brought right up to the edge of the buildings. They nevertheless stand well on their own, presenting themselves not as the necklace of the original design but as two halves of an elegant fretted cufflink.

All this is harmonious and satisfying. The imaginative part is, for the rest, to have left well alone – all the houses on Bevington Road to the north, four round the corner on the Banbury Road, and a group to the south. Everywhere institutional formality subsides into a delightful domestic confusion proper to the back sides of middle-class Victorian housing. Dividing boundary walls have been left and gates punched through. The long narrow gardens have been kept and are maintained. Everything is to scale and everything is different, full of rich textures and small surprises. The Bevington group is especially fine; the road is on the site of an old gravel pit, hence the houses are set below the level of the main quadrangle and the effect created is of a succession of sunken courts which do much to enliven the northern edge of the college precinct.

ST ANTONY'S
COLLEGE
3B

No one can accuse St Antony's of impetuosity: thirty years after it was founded under the terms of a gift (£1,250,000) from M. Antonin Besse of Aden, only one building – dining-hall, common rooms, and some teaching rooms – of a proposed collegiate group has been erected. The site originally belonged to an Anglican convent for women and the existing buildings were kept. That may have impeded further development and if so their survival is to be regretted. They are Victorian (1866–8), grim and uninviting, and not very easy to adapt for academic use; the chapel has been converted to a library and is distinctly makeshift.

Some distance away, in the middle of the site and looking a bit lost, is the new block (1968–9), concrete mounted on blue brick. The hall is on the first floor and extends through the second; it is hung with bright oriental carpets which strike an unexpectedly cheerful note.

ST BARNABAS
4A

Thomas Combe (1797–1872), Superintendent of the Clarendon Press, patron of the Pre-Raphaelites (after his death his widow presented Holman Hunt's *Light of the World* to Keble in his memory, William Morris saw his

first Pre-Raphaelite painting in his house), built St Barnabas at the end ◀
his life to serve the community that had grown up around the Clarendc
Press after its removal to the outskirts of ◀he city in 1830.

Combe's requirements that the church be solidly built, with coloure◀
decoration of the wall surfaces inside, but no money to be wasted on ▮
external appearance, were met by A. W. Blomfield's Italian-Byzanti▮
design after the style of the island cathedral of Torcello in the Veni
Lagoon. A high nave and chancel with free-standing bell tower (lat
joined to accommodate the organ), apses both east (baldacchino a▮
gorgeous gold leaf) and west (baptistery in wood), with brilliant colour
the mosaic work of the spandrels in the north arcade and the painted frie◀
of martyrs, prophets, apostles, and angels above.

John Betjeman has written an enthusiastic poem in its praise: 'Go◀
Lord, as the angelus floats down the road/Byzantine St Barnabas, ▮
Thine Abode'. Its tower is prominent in the Oxford skyline.

ST BARTHOLOMEW'S
CHAPEL

Something of a surprise once it has been tracked down: head out on Cow▮
Road and take the lane on the left after Southfield Road, leading to Or
College playing fields.

A fourteenth-century chapel with a simple whitewashed interior, part
a leper hospital far enough out in the country to be used by Oriel College,
whom it was given by Edward III in 1328, as a retreat in times of plague.
is still distinctly rural, approached down a lane between hedges, with
adjacent farmhouse, and beyond the chapel the range of the origi▮
hospital, rebuilt in the seventeenth century. In the Middle Ages the cha▮
possessed enviable relics including the skin of St Bartholomew.

ST BENET'S HALL
4B

The Oxford house of the Benedictines of Ampleforth.

ST CATHERINE'S
COLLEGE
5E

It took nearly fifty years to liberate the modern idiom in architecture
Oxford and although there are other excellent examples, its purest ar▮
with one or two exceptions – the President's Lodgings at Corpus, the
John's 'Beehives', and Powell and Moya's Brasenose infill – its earli◀
expression, is found in St Catherine's which was begun in 1960 a▮
completed in 1964. Oxford colleges have long histories and growth in ti:
is by accretion; architectural harmony has been as often as not the result
indifference or happy accident. Achievement by design – which is w▮
the college's choice of Arne Jacobsen, the Danish architect, for the ▮
implied – is not something that the Oxford mind has much experience
nor feels very comfortable with.

Jacobsen's vision was of a composition informed by rational princip
and in a resolutely secular mode, even to the exclusion of a chapel – ▮
near-by church of St Cross serves as occasion demands. The result is ▮
most rigorously disciplined expression of an architectural idea unburder
by eccentricity or debilitating 'charm' that Oxford has ever had
submit to.

St Catherine's College, hall

One of the truths that Jacobsen pressed on the Oxford consciousness w
that the relationship between buildings is as important as the buildin
themselves and it is in this that the brilliant success of his design is mc
obvious. The internal balance of the group is, fifteen years aft
completion, immaculate. What at first chilled with its hard chastity h
been reduced by time and nature to a richly satisfying mixture of texture
What Jacobsen saw and his detractors (there were many) did not was t
way in which imaginative planting would invade his precisely calculat
spaces and soften the geometrical clarity of horizontals and verticals wh
not compromising the purity of the design.

It is most apparent in the central space inside the entrance to the ma
court (the Cambridge usage seems right here). The large circular lawn h
two conifers offset, one taller than the other, giving a slightly diffused a
visually complicating focus; to the left the massive blank wall of t
dining-hall (the gift of the Esso Corporation, and the largest hall at eith
Oxford or Cambridge) is covered with a carpet of Virginia creeper an
rapidly growing vine; to the right the bronze panels of the Wolfson Libra
at first-floor level subtly and unevenly weathered; sharp right towards t
corridor between the library and the long entrance (west) front, t
rhythmical alternation of hedges and brick walls, closely set and parallel
one another like the fins of a radiator (Jacobsen's device for defining
spaces without disengaging them), allows the eye to penetrate between
the relaxed and natural planting beyond.

The library, the Bernard Sunley Theatre, and the 21-metre (70-ft) high concrete bell tower in its open 'piazza', are set centrally between the two long residential blocks which as the east and west limits of the quadrangle in effect frame the college, and in the area between the library group and the east range (i.e. that furthest away from the river) the planting is at its most successful, with low spreading heaths and heathers interspersed with massed lavender, potentillas, peonies, hypericum, iris, and other shrubs. It is all most imaginative and resourceful, and, of course, designed by Jacobsen himself. Beyond the quadrangle (which is over 60 metres (600 ft) long) the unyielding line of roof and sky is fretted and qualified by the arc of the trees which encircle the site.

The conception is powerful and it is a conception wholly realized. The detailing throughout is fastidious – perhaps most noticeably in the purpose-made bricks, the absolute uniformity of the flagstones in the paving employed for all the outside public areas, and the precision of the masons' work.

Pleasure is occasionally eroded by small failures. The entrance from Manor Road is a disappointment. The backs of the houses which look over the arm of the Cherwell alongside which the college is built are messy in a backs-of-houses way; they diminish the visual impact of the entrance façade and the moat-like water-garden behind which it is set, and that of the carefully anomalous hexagonal Music Room at the south end of the range. Residents' bicycles are provided for in a roundhouse beside the

117

pedestrian entrance road, but no provision is made for visitors' bikes and they litter the small terminal forecourt. The dining-hall is worthy of the most ceremonial occasion but doesn't seem quite apt for breakfast cerea and toast. The sculptures by Barbara Hepworth (entrance front) and the bust of Einstein by Jacob Epstein (near the bell tower) would dominate their own space almost anywhere else in Oxford. Here they look apologeti and decorative. Which in its way is a striking affirmation of the magnitud of Jacobsen's *architectural* achievement.

ST CLEMENT   Displaced from the Plain in 1828, and rebuilt among the open fields of medieval St Clement's. It is a thorough piece of Normanizing an incorporates glass from the old city church of St Martin, Carfax (gone).

ST CLEMENT'S   Until the middle of the nineteenth century the area east of Magdale
7E   Bridge remained largely undeveloped. Beyond the little country church of St Clement (demolished) which stood on the site of the Plain, the Iffle and Cowley Roads ran through open countryside and the area betwee the London Road and the River Cherwell had only scattered building the most notable of which was Stone's Almshouses, a long, grave rang of 1700.

     Today St Clement's is dominated by the Florey Building of the Queen College (James Stirling, 1968–70), a massive red-tile and glass buildin five sides of an irregular polygon open to the River Cherwell. Approache from St Clement's past a municipal car-park it looks like the corner of football stadium, with its monumental external staircase towers, and se atop pairs of concrete legs beneath which an encircling wall runs. Insic five storeys, all glazed, stepped back one behind the other, enclose a tile platform, encased by a massive tiled balustrade overlooking the river. I one corner a partly sunken breakfast room makes a second raised platform with a large metal venting chimney whimsically surmounted by a met weather-vane in the shape of an immense keyhole.

     The whole conception is calculated to play down the importance of detail, but unfortunately it is the detail which presses itself on th attention. The windows are framed in aluminium and the high proportic of frame to glass gives the fenestration a mean look and denies it th brilliance that all-over glazing such as this (compare Keble's Haywar Building) should have. Ten years after completion the building is wearin badly; there is a general air of dilapidation, many tiles are cracked ar stained, some are loose and constitute a hazard. It has an unloved air abou it and it is not a place to encourage a man to get out of bed in the mornin

     The Oxford Directory of 1846 records the name of B. H. Blackwell 46 High Street, St Clement's, among the twenty-two booksellers then business in the city. The strain of combining his business with the post of first City Librarian led to his death at the age of 42.

     The Port Mahon public house was for a time frequented by a group of poets including Louis MacNeice and Dylan Thomas. The Elm Tr

1

Tavern at the corner of Cowley Road and Jeune Street represents H. T. Hare, architect of Oxford Town Hall, in a domestic key.

ST CROSS
5E

Aisled village church with west tower, left high and dry by the encroaching University and bypassing traffic, all in the last twenty years. Bits of the original twelfth-century building remain. Dark chancel and delicately painted nave ceiling: rows of IHS monograms amidst foliage alternating with rows of suns, between chevron-edged rafters with a single central rosette. To the north of the chancel arch is a niche for a relic of the True Cross.

Originally a chapel of St Peter-in-the-East, it now doubles as the chapel for St Catherine's College and contains a memorial for the college's dead from two World Wars.

ST CROSS COLLEGE
5E

A graduate college for men and women, chiefly scientists, founded in 1965. It occupies a Victorian schoolhouse with a wooden annexe, a lawn with picnic tables and a good view of the boundary wall of Magdalen Deer Park, and a new car-park.

ST EBBE
7B

A dull church despite its long history (it dates from before 1141). Heavily Victorianized and recently scrubbed and refurbished as the price for survival in the Westgate development, in which it is a peaceful enclave.

ST EDMUND HALL
6D

The only survivor of scores of medieval halls, the rest driven out of business by the colleges, an early tradition connects the site with St Edmund of Abingdon, the only canonized Oxford scientist (1248). Only one other college (Lincoln) can offer the elegiac pleasures of a fully furnished graveyard within the precincts: the adjacent city church of St Peter-in-the-East was recently incorporated after closure and became the college library. As a result Teddy Hall is the only college in either Oxford or Cambridge with Norman architecture (nave, chancel, crypt).

The accession adds greatly to the dignity of what was always an intimate and pretty college. The Front Quad is one of the delights of an Oxford summer with its festoons of wisteria, massed petunias, window-boxes, and laurel. Beyond, in the new (Upper) quadrangle (1968–70) cobbled out of a popular dance-hall and other commercial properties on the High Street the charming vision fades. The new dining-hall replacing the original match box on Queen's Lane is meet and sufficient enough but not more. The two quadrangles are separated by a very stylish and urbane building of about 1680 on the ground floor of which is, quite disconcertingly, the chapel. Not always open, it has good Burne-Jones and Morris glass and a strong altar-piece by Ceri Richards. Well treed and all in proportion except for the large, surprised, unbalanced robinia in the Front Quad.

ST EDWARD'S SCHOOL

Founded in New Inn Hall Street 1863, removed to Summertown 1873.

ST GILES
4B

A country church which originally stood at the northern limits of the city, :
lies stranded on the peninsula which separates the tidal traffic of th
Woodstock and Banbury Roads. Despite a good deal of nineteenth- an
twentieth-century doctoring it has kept its character, a humble and sel
sufficient place not discountenanced by its grander neighbour St Aloysius.

ST GILES'
5C

St Giles' is a thoroughly enjoyable street. Design plays no part in it: the tw
sides wander along in an inconsequential way and only the Randolph Hot
and the Taylorian Institute on the west and on the east St Giles' Hous
(no. 16) display any real self-confidence. And while these are very sel
confident indeed they are not well enough sited to pull the street togethe
architecturally. Few of the other buildings are anything special. Wh:
delights is the spaciousness – the liberating effect of buildings, trees, an
sky in harmony. It is a pleasure that no other street in Oxford offers.

ST HILDA'S
COLLEGE
8E

St Hilda's, the latest of the four women's colleges (founded 1893), occupi
a matchless site stretching along the east bank of the Cherwell south
Magdalen Bridge, with lawns falling away to the river and views ov
Magdalen College School playing fields to the towers and spires of t
University beyond. The original building is a handsome late eighteent
century house (unfortunately with later additions to north and sout
which belonged to John Sibthorp, Sherardian Professor of Botany, bu
within sight of his Botanic Garden. That house sets a standard that eve
subsequent addition has failed to live up to.

A series of Victorian and twentieth-century architects from Deane ar
Woodward (1862) to Sir Albert Richardson (1961), mesmerized perha
by the site's pastoral charms, have designed buildings which offer litt
more than good views of the Cherwell. Alison and Peter Smithson's Gard
Building (1968–70) is set at a resolute distance from the river, as though
avoid its blandishments, and is a plain protest against the timidity of t
others: square, four storey, glass and concrete, with chamfered corne
and constructions of diagonally braced timber attached to the outside
the building and running round the top three storeys at floor lev
unequivocally decorative, and imparting a strong rhythm to an otherwi
unassertive façade.

ST HUGH'S
COLLEGE
2C

Not content with the Principalship of one women's college, Miss Elizabe
Wordsworth, grand-niece of the poet and daughter of a bishop, in 18:
founded a second, St Hugh's, as a hostel for students too poor to afforc
place at Lady Margaret Hall, over which she presided. By 1916 it h
established itself on its present site an uncomfortable distance up t
Banbury Road. An assortment of run-of-the-mill institutional red-bri
buildings of no distinction, it turns its only presentable face away from t
street front.

Architecturally it is redeemed by the graceful coda of David Robert
Wolfson Building (1964–6), a low serpentine block, added as an extensi

to the existing college buildings in the direction of the Woodstock Road. The north face is simple and unfussy (and quite free from the chilly formality of Roberts's earlier Sacher Building at New College), the south is broken by recessed upper storeys and balconies and the fierce brick softened by good marginal planting – wisteria, Virginia creeper, laurel, and massed lavender and rosemary. Some distance away on the garden side (also by Roberts and built first) a large keep-like building saved from monumentality by the spaciousness of the sunken terrace from which it rises and the clever detailing of its raked sides which result in a blunted arrow shape as seen from the south.

In the hall there is a portrait of the celebrated Charlotte Moberly, the first Principal of the college, who in 1901 during a walk in the great park of the Palace of Versailles claimed to have stepped out of the twentieth and into the eighteenth century and to have found herself in the company of Marie Antoinette, a story which as might be expected of a daughter of a Bishop of Salisbury and the sister of a Regius Professor of Pastoral Theology, she stuck to, and about which she published a book.

ST JOHN EVANGELIST
8E

The mother church of the Society of St John Evangelist, an Anglican monastic order of mission priests popularly known as the Cowley Fathers, founded in 1865, and the oldest Anglican Society for men religious; now constituted in three Congregations – English, American, and Canadian.

Outside it is a strong, unhesitant design with no concession to mere display except the obelisks which cap the flying buttresses to the aisles; and they are fitting in their geometrical simplicity. The west tower is full of a chaste dignity and deserves its prominent exposure to the Iffley Road. Inside a joyful painted ceiling running the full length of the church, interrupted twice by transverse arches which correspond to flying buttresses on the outside. The organ case is painted, and so are the ceilings of the aisles and tower. There is a rood screen beyond which is the choir with elegant stalls.

The church is by G. F. Bodley, 1894–1902, as is the adjoining Mission House and chapel on Marston Street.

ST JOHN STREET
5B

Early Victorian residential street of stone houses, much discoloured, with pretensions to elegance spoiled by fidgety and inconsistent detail.

ST JOHN'S COLLEGE
5C

It is no accident that St John's and Trinity were founded in the same year, 1555. The accession to the throne of Mary Tudor in 1553 with her promise of restoring England to Roman Catholicism after the Protestant heresies of Henry VIII and his son Edward must have seemed to adherents of the old religion like prayers answered; and the foundation of St John's by Sir Thomas White and Trinity by Sir Thomas Pope were acts of thanksgiving.

Pope had withdrawn from public life during Edward VI's reign because of his opposition to the government's reforming zeal, but returned as a privy councillor on Mary's accession. White had remained a Roman

121

Catholic and his statutes for St John's declare his interest 'to strengthen the orthodox faith, in so far as it is weakened by the damage of time and the malice of men'. And no doubt both saw the appropriateness of acquiring, for the purpose of their new foundations, monastic colleges which had failed to survive the dissolution of the monasteries – Benedictine Durham College in the case of Trinity, and St Bernard's College, a Cistercian house, in the case of St John's.

Trinity, notwithstanding agreeable freaks like Dr Bathurst, President of Trinity from 1664 to 1704, who used to throw stones from his garden at the windows of Balliol, or Walter Savage Landor who discharged a gun at the rooms of a man whom he hated for his Toryism, has always been an easygoing and fun-loving college. St John's, infected perhaps by the spiritual zeal and entrepreneurial ambition of its Founder (he was a Merchant Taylor and a successful business man), has always cultivated a much more belligerent style. Two of its early Presidents were deprived for refusing to take the Oath of Supremacy. Edmund Campion, one of its original Fellows, died a Jesuit and a martyr. The counter-reforming William Laud, President of St John's 1611–21, as Archbishop of Canterbury under Charles I took on Puritanism and the Long Parliament and lost. Nearer our own day A. E. Housman has plied a desperate hook in defence of classical scholarship, the poet Robert Graves in defence of anything that took his fancy, and Mr Dean Rusk as U.S. Secretary of State has waged holy war in defence of 'western values', aided and abetted by Kingsley Amis. St John's men all.

It is a relief that nothing of this truculence carries over into the college itself. The fifteenth-century gate-tower and the north extension along St Giles' by George Gilbert Scott the younger (1881) is a familiar pattern of late Gothic with late Victorian additions. The fifteenth century, i.e. the Cistercian buildings, continues in the Front Quad, two storeys, fortunately never added to. Hall and chapel fill the north side. There is nothing medieval in the chapel except some English embroidered work in the Baylie chapel on the north side – part of a large collection of early (pre-Reformation) ecclesiastical vestments some of them apparently the Founder's gift; everything else Victorian. The hall is largely eighteenth century, plastered and panelled, but with a stone screen, unusual for its date (1742).

Canterbury Quad beyond is all Laud's work (1631–6) except for the south range containing the library, built at the end of the sixteenth century out of timber and stone salvaged from Beaumont Palace. North and south ranges repeat each other as do east and west. East and west have slender round-headed arcades stopped at the ends; in the middle and above the most sumptuous decorative centre-pieces organized around bronze statues of Charles I (east) and his queen Henrietta Maria (west); the north and south are plain in comparison but have nicely carved string courses to offset the severity of the battlements. Canterbury Quad is unremittingly stylish – taut yet animated, luxuriant without a hint of vulgarity, and the whole

Opposite: St John's College, Canterbury Quad

12.

thing well grounded by the domestic gravity of the President's Lodgings in the north range.

An archway leads to the gardens which do much to relax the mind. About 2 hectares (5 acres) of them running through to Parks Road in the east. An early nineteenth-century guide-book describes them as 'originally disposed in that formal, rectilinear taste, which Kent, Brown, and Repton have successively combined to destroy'. Formal geometry, that is, superseded by 'serpentine walks', quincunxes (St John's had one) by lawns and herbaceous borders. It is Oxford's closest accommodation to the English Country House Garden, rich variegated beds, always threatening untidiness, never succumbing to it.

A nice, a very nice touch, reveals itself only to the nosy: the border surrounding the lawns of the President's walled garden are given over to vegetables.

St John's is well off for space and in the last twenty years has used it imaginatively. The North Quad behind the St Giles' front has a mix of decent buildings of many dates, 1640 to 1930, obviously added as needed. It is worth visiting for the 'Beehives' designed by the Architects Co Partnership, 1958–60, which mark Oxford's first real break with nervous antiquarianism. It is a severely regimented range, surprising rather than adventurous – the adventure lies in the doing it at all – and it doesn't grow on one. But it showed Oxford the way to more satisfying designs in the sixties.

One of these is the new Sir Thomas White Quad which fills the large space between North Quad and Museum Road. In fact, it is of 1974–7 but it is by Arup Associates and obviously a development of their Somerville buildings ten years earlier. The same effect of a cellular pre-cast concrete frame containing fully glazed façades, but much more varied than Somerville. A single continous range round two sides of a garden which is on two levels, it is the most ambitious addition to a college since the Second World War and one of the most successful. In its disciplined vigour it is worthy successor to Canterbury Quad.

ST MARGARET
2B

A gloomy church (1883–93), with a carefully decorative interior.

ST MARY MAGDALEN
6C

A spacious church, wider than it is long (with north and south aisles and south chapel each as wide as the nave); much rebuilt, finally by Sir George Gilbert Scott (in 1842), who did away with the remaining Norman bits. A restless and cluttered interior. Some poor Victorian glass, a very decorative fourteenth-century font. Modern memorial tablet to John Aubrey (1626–97), the seventeenth-century gossip and antiquarian, on the west wall of the south chapel.

**ST MARY
THE VIRGIN**
6C

It is always hard to disassociate Oxford buildings from the people who inhabited them and of none is this more true than St Mary's. It is still thought of in Oxford as Newman's church: it was here that he effectively ended his career in the Anglican Church and Oxford, originally in bitterness later with pride, has never forgotten that.

It began life as a parish church in the eleventh century – no part of which survives – and a parish church it still is; but for nearly 400 years when the University had scarcely a building to call its own St Mary's was at the centre of its corporate life. The different Faculties met in different parts of it to conduct their business while the Congregation of all the Faculties met first in the choir and later in the Congregation House, a separate building attached to the north side of the church; the University Library was housed in a room above the Congregation House until 1488; the Chancellor's Court met in Adam de Brome's chapel on the north side of the nave until 1646; the annual 'Act' when new masters were admitted to the body of University teachers was held in the nave until the building of the Sheldonian in 1669. St Mary's must have been the Rialto of medieval and Reformation Oxford and no doubt much like St Paul's cathedral in London, a place for 'bargains, meetings, murders, conspiracies, and ordinary payment of money'.

A crossroads too. Certainly for Newman, who recognized the impossibility of his Anglican faith there even if he did not at once accept the inevitability of Rome. More dramatically, more pathetically, for Thomas Cranmer, Henry VIII's supple Archbishop of Canterbury, the first Primate of Protestant England; brought to Oxford with his fellow bishops Latimer and Ridley to defend himself against charges of heresy during Queen Mary's vindictive reign, he was tried in the choir of St Mary's and sentenced in the nave, going to the stake from there after repudiating his earlier recantations. It was at the very spot where Cranmer suffered his final degradations (beside 'Cranmer's pillar', its moulding damaged in the construction of the dais on which he sat) that Newman used to kneel before climbing the pulpit opposite.

Few buildings have so various a character or define it so clearly for us as St Mary's. Different parts of it seem to have developed, by a strange calculus of history and habitual use, quite independent personalities and moods. The chancel with its plain weathered fifteenth-century panelling, a single row of stalls, and high windows with clear glass, is like an East Anglian church in its lightness and simplicity. The nave is a much more robust place: double decked ranges of Perpendicular windows in aisles and clerestory, the roof with a close-set grid of timbers painted alternately red and white, the black-and-white lozenges of the marble floor, the open central space between the north and south porches like a great waiting room; nave fifteenth century, with a west gallery and the Vice-Chancellor's throne of 1828. The north aisle chapel, built by Adam de Brome, founder of Oriel College, c.1328, and with his tomb, is fitted with seventeenth-century panelling and a second Vice-Chancellor's throne, and is altogether severer; in 1733 it was walled off from the rest of the church to protect the heads of colleges from draughts. The Congregation House (c.1320–30) is of two storeys; homely rooms turned to a variety of uses since the Univer-

Opposite: St Peter-in-the-East
and Queen's from New College
garden

sity relinquished them – the lower room has been store room, powd
magazine, schoolhouse, fire station, lecture room, chapel, parish hall, ar
now (1979) a Brass Rubbing Centre, open seven days a week, and one
the busiest places in Oxford on a July afternoon.

The exterior is dominated by the great tower (late thirteenth centur
with its cathedral spire. The spire has gabled and crocketted openings
four faces, between each pair tall pinnacles with twin gables, each gab
with compounded pinnacles; at the corners of the tower buttresses risi
above the pierced parapet with canopied niches and statues inserted and
covered with the most profuse ball-and-flower ornament. Nothing
Oxford is remotely like it and not many things in England are. The sou
porch by Nicholas Stone (1637) is Baroque and handsome.

**ST MICHAEL-AT-
THE-NORTH-GATE**
6C

Its Anglo-Saxon tower, the oldest building in Oxford, marks the northe
limit of the medieval city. The North Gate adjoining was demolished
1772 together with the Bocardo prison above it from which the Protesta
martyrs Latimer and Ridley went to the stake in Broad Street in 1555.

The interior is undistinguished but a recent white paint job has dis
pated some of the urban ecclesiastical gloom. Excellent late thirteen
century glass in the east window. In the vestry is kept a stone-carved 'ero
female figure' (so the inspector for the Royal Commission on Histori
Monuments describes it), apparently a pre-Christian fertility fetish, whi
may be seen by appointment.

**ST MICHAEL'S
STREET**
6B

It has a couple of substantial stone houses – one (no. 20) with mark
pretensions – the Oxford Union, and a framed view of the tower and spi
of Wesley Memorial Church which makes it more elegant than, when se
with the rest of the front, it is.

ST PAUL
4B

This modest Greek revival church (1836) with its fluted columns a
restrained façade has a special claim on the affections because for ma
years a contented ruin in this relentlessly restored city. It is now bei
renovated and it is impossible not to mourn the loss of its scrofulc
elegance behind massed weeds and hollyhocks and fine wrought-ir
railings.

**ST PETER-
IN-THE-EAST**
6D

In Pevsner's judgement 'without doubt the most interesting church
Oxford', so it is a pity that it has been taken over by St Edmund Hall a
library and a greater pity that most of the interest is in the interior. Lots
energetic Norman decoration well supported by later features. On
outside varied windows and tracery. The crypt can be viewed.

**ST PETER'S
COLLEGE**
6B

Occupies the site of the medieval New Inn Hall which was merged wi
Balliol in 1887. Forty years later F. J. Chavasse, retired Bishop
Liverpool (he had earlier been Rector of the church of St Peter-le-Bail
now the college chapel), promoted the idea of a new college for poo

1

undergraduates, especially those who might be encouraged to take order
in the Church of England. He died in the year the college was founded
(1928) but it remains a witness to his idea and a memorial to him and his
family. In the chapel Chavasse is celebrated by a large memorial (a plaster
cast of the front panel of his tomb in Liverpool cathedral), a stained glass
window, and a pulpit; the family by the grave of one son (first Master of the
college), and memorials to two others and his wife, as well as to two more
remote Chavasses. And a glass case on a college stairway displays a citation
in honour of his son Noel, a hero of the First World War, together with his
military decorations which include not one but two Victoria Crosses.

All of which takes some living up to and the college doesn't do it very
well. The good part is the former Rectory of St Peter-le-Bailey, an honest
Georgian house; the chapel itself (Basil Champneys, 1874) is dull. It is a
great misfortune that the early years of the college coincided with the most
unimaginative period for architecture in Oxford's history, and the first
three buildings (1929–53) are random and lumpish Queen Anne in style;
twenty years later not much has improved and the two buildings of 1970
and 1972 (Matthews and Latner) are half-hearted gestures toward
'modernism' – a pity when so much good modern work was going up all
around. The Master's Lodgings lie behind the college on the other side of
Bulwarks Lane and once housed the offices of the Oxford Canal Company,
a rather grand Grecian building (1827–9) with portico, Doric columns
and a pretty sunken garden.

**ST PHILIP AND
ST JAMES**
2B

A church of immense aplomb with all the credentials: tower and a very
solidly set and strong spire, prominent in all views of the north Oxford
skyline – on a May afternoon in 1866, the year the spire was built, Gerard
Manley Hopkins saw it from Cumnor Hill 'through blue haze rising pale :
a pink light'; nave and aisles with clerestory, transepts, vaulted apse, rose
windows; bands of pink sandstone on the outside, piers of pink granite and
black marble inside (G. E. Street, 1860–6). It is a very confident Victorian
prescription for a burgeoning north Oxford, and it still fits.

**ST THOMAS
THE MARTYR**
6A

Founded in 1141 by Osney Abbey but passed to Christ Church at the
Reformation, which explains why Robert Burton's arms are over the door
of the south porch: he was a Student of Christ Church and was made vicar
of St Thomas in 1616; while he held the living he published his *Anatomy of
Melancholie* (1621).

Restored in the nineteenth century, the only good bits are the priest's
door on the south of the chancel, thirteenth century with original iron
scrollwork; the brass chandelier (1705), the oldest in the city; the self-
possessed vicarage on the north side (1893).

Becket Street is railway country and from the pretty, unkempt churchyard the view is of a motor-car graveyard.

1

SCIENCE AREA
4D

Occupies a crowded site on the south side of the University Parks an‹ without a single building of any distinction, it is best seen from a car drive‹ moderately fast.

SHELDONIAN THEATRE
6C

A theatre in a literal though limited sense – it was built (1663–9) t‹ accommodate the University's full-dress ceremonial occasions. The mos‹ important of these is Encaenia – formerly known as 'the Act' – the annu‹ celebration of benefactors and honorary degree giving. Encaenia ha‹ previously been held in the University church of St Mary the Virgin but i‹ post-Restoration Oxford the prejudice against secular business bein‹ carried on in consecrated buildings was sharp. A separate Theatre wa‹ decided on and Gilbert Sheldon, Archbishop of Canterbury and forme‹ Warden of All Souls, agreed to pay for it – though he refused to attend i‹ opening and declared his intention never to see it, nor did he.

The commission went to Christopher Wren, an astronomer and amateu‹ architect. Wren, then only 31, found the pattern of his design in th‹ Roman theatre and a somewhat idiosyncratic version of a Roman theatr‹ (adapted for a northern climate, since Roman theatres were roofless) . what he produced. The façade is classical but faces south, away from th‹ street, and it is the semicircular back which the eye usually sees. That is ‹ pity because the back is architecturally much less firmly realized than th‹ front. Wren is not altogether to blame; a rebuild of the roof in 1800– which swept away his crown of prominent barrel-like dormers (eac‹ surmounted by a bishop's mitre) and the replacement of his lantern in 183‹ by a much larger one has unbalanced and weakened the back elevatio‹ the fine, carved north doorway which must have acted as an expressi‹ focus of the powerful rhythms of the original composition now loo‹ uncomfortable in a façade that is too placid for it.

The inside is all brown and gilt like a giant chocolate box. An open flo‹ is surrounded by steeply pitched benches and a lofty gallery supported ‹ wooden pillars pretending to be marble. The painted ceiling (by Robe‹ Streater, Serjeant Painter to Charles II) illustrates the triumph of Arts an‹ Science over Envy, Rapine, and 'brutish scoffing Ignorance', and aimir‹ at apocalypse achieves prettiness. The Vice-Chancellor's throne faces t‹ great south processional door, which has the organ over; the Procto‹ pulpits to right and left sport lion's heads with mouths full of *fasces*. T‹ climb to the lantern is rewarded by the best views of Oxford and (to t‹ surprise of many) surrounding hills. Until 1713 the Sheldonian also hous‹ the University Press; books were set up in type in the rooms beneath t‹ galleries, they were printed in the basement and stored in the attics.

The line of monumental sculptured heads along the Broad Stre‹ boundary wall (renewed in 1867 and again in 1972) was intended by Wr‹ to recall the Antique boundary-stones known as 'herms' or 'terms', whic‹ were often ornamented with human features. The heads figure patheticall‹ in Max Beerbohm's *Zuleika Dobson*.

1

SHIP STREET
6C

Not quite flat, not quite straight, not at all busy; the best confection of domestic, commercial, and collegiate use in Oxford. Stopped at the Turl end by Exeter College and Sir George Gilbert Scott's needle spire on the nineteenth-century chapel (the only good view of it) with a handsome and unexpected chestnut tree in Jesus College bicycle yard overhanging.

SHOTOVER HILL

Ancient common, full of gorse and hawthorn, criss-crossed by paths, and the best walking country near Oxford, it has an invigorating sense of fresh air and freedom that Oxford nowhere else provides. Until the nineteenth century the road from Oxford to London ran across it.

SOMERVILLE COLLEGE
4B

Somerville was founded in 1879 as an alternative to Lady Margaret Hall for women unable to meet the restrictive Anglican entrance requirements of Lady Margaret Hall which opened its doors in that year, and Somerville has been trying, more or less convincingly, ever since to prove the superiority of non-denominationalism. It has a reputation for high-mindedness and worldly success, numbering amongst its old members, besides numerous scholars of great distinction (including one Nobel Laureate), best-selling novelists (Dorothy Sayers and Iris Murdoch), social reformers (Margaret Fry, Eleanor Rathbone, Barbara Ward), politicians (Shirley Williams, Eirene White); and Mrs Margaret Thatcher.

The college lies between the Radcliffe Infirmary and Little Clarendon Street, the Woodstock Road and Walton Street, with the entrance on the Woodstock Road. Two rather suffocated quadrangles must be got through to reach the main quadrangle with its lawns, trees, and space to breathe. The library to the north is a late job of Basil Champneys (1902–3) and a tired one, though there is a touch of Champneys's stylishness in the (glazed) loggia and the nicely balanced oriels; it looks a pleasant place to read in. To the east two large buildings (1910–13), one with the hall on the first floor. The chapel on the south stands by itself.

Somerville's claims on the casual visitor rest on the buildings of the last twenty-five years, especially the range along Little Clarendon Street which is no doubt where the casual visitor will approach it from. The Vaughan Building and the Margery Fry–Elisabeth Nuffield Building (Philip Dowson of Arup Associates, 1958–66) run parallel to and set back from Little Clarendon Street; they are long elegant ranges which give the impression of being suspended inside a cellular concrete frame like some elaborate building toy. From the inside of the quadrangle they are seen to be mounted on a high platform of dark-grey brick and this anchors them in a rather spoil-sporty way. The view from the street which conceals the platform is much better. Fry–Nuffield in particular, seen behind the canopied arcade of shops built against it at street level, and bobbing above the arcade, is a great pleasure. And it is a reminder of something not altogether to the University's credit: that this is the only piece of collegiate building since the Second World War that has enhanced rather than diminished the urban life of the area upon which it has been imposed.

131

On the south side of the main quadrangle and completing it is Wolfson Building (Philip Dowson again, 1968), a powerful, raw-boned statement in glass and concrete flanked by two windowless brick towers with raked tops which look as though they have strayed from the bottom of someone's garden. Fifteen years on it still provides a visual shock in such a genteel context. Smaller surprises are a Caroesque steel construction at the opposite end of the quadrangle, and the industrial smoke-stack in the yard of the Radcliffe Infirmary to the north.

SOUTH PARADE With characteristic Oxford logic it lies north of North Parade on the Banbury Road. A rather nasty but useful strip of commercial development, it is an early type of the suburban shopping plaza.

THE SYNAGOGUE
5A

A Jewish community was already established in Oxford by 1141, and though never large, it flourished until the expulsion of the Jews from England in 1290. They settled, as was their habit in the Middle Ages, in the centre of the city, as convenient for business, and the Oxford Jewry lay on both sides of St Aldate's (then called Great Jewry or the King's Jewry), especially the west side between Carfax and Pembroke Street and on the east in the neighbourhood of the north front of Christ Church – the synagogue actually lying in what is now the north-west corner of Tom Quad. The Jewish cemetery or 'Jews' Garden' lay outside the East Gate on the site of the Botanic Garden and extending north to include the High Street front of Magdalen College and Tower. In the Middle Ages they were especially active as financiers and included at least four women in business on their own account – Regina, Henna, Chera, and one Belaset, who was a considerable business woman and had a hand in transactions as far away as Wiltshire.

The present synagogue is a new building in Nelson Street, Jericho, not far from St Barnabas's church. It fits well into a difficult site between a group of modest Victorian terrace houses and a long row of nineteenth-century artisans' cottages. It is a low brick building with an asymmetrical pitched roof, a neat entrance courtyard of four bays with canopies, behind a steel gate. Simple, unaffected, affirmative.

TACKLEY'S INN
6C

Williams and Glyns Bank. Not much to look at but it conceals a medieval hall.

**TAYLORIAN
INSTITUTE**
5B

See ASHMOLEAN MUSEUM.

THORNTON'S
6C

The last of the familiar, shabby, Oxford bookshops. Claustrophobia on four floors, neat and orderly below, running away into narrow staircases and ill-lit rooms stacked high with second-hand books. There is still a Mr Thornton.

133

SECOND HAND   HISTORY ECONOMICS & POLITICS LAW   ANTHROPOLOGY ENGLISH LIT. POETRY MATHS.   OXF. CLASS. TEXTS GEOGRAPHY FICTION EVERYMAN LIB.   FIRST FLOOR

SECOND FLOOR

THEOLOGY PHILOSOPHY AFRICANA SCIENCE MEDICINE FRENCH GERMAN

You are INVITED to INSPECT the STOCK UPSTAIRS

TOWN HALL
7C

Civic collegiate, by H. T. Hare (1893–7), and yard for yard the most uninhibited façade in Oxford; it does more than enough to assert the dignity of the city against the University. Renaissance if anything and gorgeous. The effervescence of the top storey with its gables, towers, arches, cupolas, pillars, pinnacles, parapets, and chimneys leaves Queen Victoria, whose statue stands in the middle of it, looking very apprehensive.

Inside a grand staircase leads to a big hall with aisles and gallery, and arcading above and below. Quantities of Jacobean plasterwork badly in need of refurbishing. The council chamber is small but handsome, crowded with sensible Victorian desks, and a public gallery contained by two strong arches opens on to it.

In the corridor outside, an unexpectedly good collection of watercolours by a painter to whom even Oxford, with its appetite for overpraising modest achievements (and as a judicious corollary, underpraising great ones), has given less than his due: William Turner 'of Oxford' (1789–1851), born in the county at Black Bourton, in his later years he conducted a drawing school at his house in St John Street, where he also had a small garden in which he grew plants 'suitable for introduction in the foregrounds of his pictures'.

TOWN WALL

Oxford was in the Middle Ages a completely walled city, and today, though it is no York or Chester, there are considerable remains, viewable at a number of places. None of the six gates remains except in name.

The line of the wall ran from the North Gate at St Michael's Street, crossed New Inn Hall Street at the Wesley Memorial Church, linking up with the Norman ditch of the Castle at Bulwarks Lane. East of the North Gate it followed a line south of Broad Street, crossing the Turl just north of Exeter chapel, then across the south face of the Sheldonian (outside), diagonally across the gravelled yard between the Bodleian (inside) and Clarendon Building (outside) to the gateway of the North Quad of Hertford College, where Smythgate stood. Then along a line through New College grounds and gardens, turning south at Longwall Street, crossing the High Street at the Eastgate Hotel and continuing south through Merton gardens before turning west (forming the south boundary of Merton) and across to St Aldate's (where the South Gate stood just to the north of the War Memorial Garden). West of St Aldate's it follows the line of Brewer Street, cutting through St Ebbe's to the West Gate at the junction of Church Street and Castle Street.

That is, the modern George Street, Broad Street, Holywell, and Longwall lay outside the wall; New Inn Hall Street, St Michael's Street, Ship Street, Turl Street, Catte Street, High Street, Queen Street, Cornmarket Street, the north half of St Aldate's, Merton Street, Pembroke Street, and St Ebbe's, inside.

The most complete and viewable sections are the long stretch with bastions, wall walk, battlements, etc., in the grounds of New College, the

ornton's

boundary wall of Merton facing on to Merton Fields, and the boundar‍
wall of Pembroke on the north side of Brewer Street.

TOW-PATH Good walks along the Thames upstream as far as Binsey and Godstow‍
downstream to Iffley and Sandford. Easy access from Christ Churc‍
Meadow, the stretch there still with a handful of barges, survivors of thos‍
once universally used by college boat clubs and now happily restored.

TRILL MILL An ancient watercourse which ran through St Ebbe's, largely unde‍
STREAM ground, before surfacing just south of Christ Church where it can today b‍
seen in the War Memorial Garden. In a subterranean reach of the strear‍
was found some sixty years ago the carcass of a punt with two Victoria‍
skeletons in it.

TRINITY COLLEGE Trinity's disagreement with its neighbour Balliol, inveterate, and to th‍
6C rest of the world rather boring, starts with the Broad Street front; ther‍
could be no steeper contrast than that between Waterhouse's ambitiou‍
Balliol façade and Trinity's pretty muddle of cottages flanked b‍
wrought iron and rose garden, with the handsome gables of Kettell Hall i‍
the wings.

Trinity's manorial style begins with gates on Broad Street; inside ther‍
lies not a quadrangle at all (though it is called Front Quad) but a garde‍
dense with carefully set trees and at the end of a drive, a brisk walk away,‍
gate-tower with statues (Geometry, Astronomy, Theology, Medicine)‍
which until comparatively recent times the college has treated as the re‍
entrance, approached as it was from Broad Street by a narrow roa‍
between high walls – and to the right a building with balustrading an‍
urns.

This is the chapel and though as late as 1691–4, the first non-Goth‍
chapel in Oxford. The interior is worth travelling long distances to see b‍
is not describable in terms which will do it justice. From the west end‍
presents to the eye the most lavish display of secular ornament with n‍
pretence at ecclesiastical decorum. Even the altar-piece (an inlaid panel)‍
geometrical in design and it is surrounded, in brilliant contrast, by deep‍
encrusted, deeply cut, carved wooden decoration of flowers, fruit, foliag‍
and vases, surmounted by a powerful curved pediment with urns an‍
reclining angels – or rather lounging putti. The ceiling is covered wit‍
panels of stucco filled with similar motifs surrounding painted panels, lik‍
calcified incense. The Founder and his second wife are stored in a gla‍
cupboard on the north side of the altar, as though for protection from a‍
this infectious delight.

To pass from this to Durham Quadrangle is like stepping from a thro‍
room into a stable yard. Durham Quad incorporates the surviving bits ‍
the medieval college supported by the Benedictine priory of Durham f‍
the use of its monks, which was purchased after the dissolution in 1544 ‍
Sir Thomas Pope, a civil servant with good connections, and re-establishe‍

1

by him as the College of the Holy and Undivided Trinity in 1555. It is a bleak place, fifteenth century on the east and housing there the old library. (Dr Johnson, a friend of Thomas Warton, Professor of Poetry and a Fellow, liked Trinity library best as a place to read. 'If a man has a mind to *prance*, he must study at Christ Church and All Souls.') The hall on the left (west) is of indeterminate age, small and dull. Its most prominent feature is a large and very bad painting entitled *Arts and Sciences at Trinity College 1977* which none of those represented in it (they include two Nobel Laureates and two holders of the Order of Merit) can be very happy about.

Furthest from Broad Street is Garden Quad which began with a good Wren building of 1668 (on the north side) subsequently messed about with (a third storey was raised), copied (on the south by the ubiquitous William Townesend, 1728), and added to (west range, 1682), and so losing all its character and looking like any old quad anywhere. The fourth side opens on to the garden which runs away in grand fashion to wrought-iron gates (models for those on Broad Street) on Parks Road. There is to one side a narrow avenue of rather weedy lime trees.

On a plinth south of Wren's building is a weathered bust of John Henry Newman who spent happy years as an undergraduate at Trinity. 'Trinity', he wrote many years later, 'had never been unkind to me; there used to be much snapdragon growing on the walls opposite my freshman's room there, and I had for years taken it as the emblem of my own perpetual residence, even unto death, in my University.'

Opening off the Garden towards Broad Street is a space surrounded on three sides by a medley of 'modern' buildings. This is Cumberbatch Quadrangle. On the west, the back of a range by T. G. Jackson (1883–7) which faces the chapel and Balliol; a building of character as is to be expected from Jackson. Opposite, the neo-classical library (1925–7) with lots of fluting, adjoined on the north by a square block which makes a feature of a spiral staircase leading to a terrace which can hardly have been worth the effort. Joining these two ranges on the south side is a small auxiliary quadrangle developed (1964–8) in collaboration with Blackwell's whose main shop lies on Broad Street just beyond. Blackwell's did rather well out of the arrangement: it resulted in a rather depressed quad for Trinity and a vast underground showroom for them. The main quadrangle has a centre-piece of decorative paving – flagstones, cobbles, bricks, circles, oblongs. Cumberbatch is a thoroughly disjointed place, a deadly example of pressing too strenuously after individuality in separate elements without reference to firm principles of design. An example of, well, Cumberbatching.

Between Jackson's range and the chapel (we are back in Front Quadrangle) the President's Lodgings also by Jackson and here he really means business. It is Jackson in his most domineering mood, Jacobean and Elizabethan motifs animated by the most colossal energy. One can only stand before it and marvel.

Trinity College, President's Lodgings

139

TURL STREET
6C

Heavily collegiate – Exeter, Jesus, Lincoln – with expressive trees at each end, that at the south against the backdrop of tower, spire, and portico of All Saints church, which deflects the Turl there and presides over it.

TURN AGAIN LANE
7B

Pre-Victorian name recently restored to what little is left of Charles Street, and appropriately bollarded against traffic at the St Ebbe's Street exit.

UNIVERSITY COLLEGE
6D

The reputation of University College in the world is the victim of a double embarrassment. For 500 years it persisted in claiming Alfred the Great as its Founder. The other embarrassment is more widely known – the ejection in 1811 of the poet Shelley when an undergraduate because he abandoned his favourite pastime of sailing paper boats long enough to publish a pamphlet entitled 'The Necessity of Atheism'. The college made amends for that somewhat belatedly by accepting from the poet's family in 1893 the monument by Onslow Ford intended for the Protestant Cemetery in Rome, where Shelley is buried, but refused by the authorities. In white marble, it represents the poet drowned on the sands of Viareggio in August 1822. As it lies, in a bleak cupola in the north-west corner of the Front Quad, it looks like the reluctant act of expiation it is. Yet it is a memorable piece, Victorian romanticism at its most mannered and least sentimental.

Behind its long High Street frontage University College has two proper quadrangles and haphazard outliers. The quadrangles represent a double hangover. The Front Quad of 1634–77 displays the late Gothic symptoms (especially noticeable in the windows) also found, for example, in the front quadrangles of Wadham and Oriel, representing conservative satisfaction with the old styles. But Radcliffe Quad of a hundred years later (1716–19) repeats them, and indeed duplicates the design of the earlier quad. To realize how eccentric this is, think of what else was being built at the same time: the Clarendon Building, Hawksmoor's North Quad at All Souls, and Peckwater Quad at Christ Church.

Both hall and chapel open off the Front Quadrangle and both have undergone characteristic nineteenth-century restorations. In the hall only the roof is original. The chapel has stained glass by the ubiquitous Abraham van Linge who also worked at the cathedral (1630s), Queen's (1635), Balliol (1637) – probably his best as it was his last set (1641), richly coloured in his usual unsubtle way, and all the better for being easy to read; a group of Flaxman monuments; and a nice uneventfully panelled reredos which doesn't quite live up to the carving of the screen and stalls – all post-Restoration.

Further east, Logic Lane, running between High Street and Merton Street, has been incorporated into the college but not very successfully: it is still a street with buildings on it and an uneasy assortment they are. At the High Street end a half-timbered job (1903) with a calculated charm which would be at home in a leafy Surrey suburb but not here – especially not next to the large range which fills the rest of the east side of Logic Lane (Goodhart Building, 1960–1). That is representative of aboriginal

Opposite: University College, Logic Lane with Queen's behind

'modernism' in Oxford when architects were struggling with a language which they had not yet mastered the idiom of. A much better, clever little number stands at the Merton Street exit. But nothing here is reconciled with the weighty Jacobean of G. F. Bodley's Master's Lodgings (1879) against which it all seems very flimsy.

A quite separate development has grown up around Sir George Gilbert Scott's library (1861) at the south-west corner of the site and best approached from Kybald Street. In turn, nineteenth-century almshouses, solid Jacobean-ish brick house (1887), a witty little brick gatehouse (John Fryman, 1968–71) which jumps across the road, with access from a cleverly contrived staircase inside the precinct wall. It stands next to a fifteenth-century archway and without a trace of awkwardness. Beyond, the library holds together a group which doesn't otherwise take itself too seriously.

The college has an unusual accumulation of indifferent statuary. Queen Anne (who displaced King Alfred) on the High Street front of the entrance gate-tower, James II on the inside; Dr John Radcliffe on the inside of the gate-tower of the quadrangle he himself paid for – a marvellously expressive piece by Francis Bird (1717) and in a different class from the rest – and Queen Mary on the exterior; King Alfred in the garden of the Master's Lodgings. In the library, looking as though the library was built around them, a colossal pair of statues of William Scott, afterwards Lord Stowell, Fellow 1765–75, and his brother and pupil John Scott, afterwards Lord Eldon, shown seated (which is just as well), made for Westminster Abbey but rejected.

UNIVERSITY MUSEUM 4C

The Museum marks the beginning of modern scientific studies at Oxford and the University went to war over it. Dr Henry Acland, Reader in Anatomy, later Regius Professor of Medicine, provided the impetus in a memorandum of 1847. Both the object and the method of carrying it out were violently opposed. If the rhetoric was impenetrable (Science, the Vice-Chancellor warned, tends to Infidelity) the tactics were not: in Convocation the motion to install gas-pipes for lighting was allowed to pass, but that to approve the purchase of gas burners was lost by two votes. In the end the issue was carried by the unlikely alliance of the progressives and Dr Pusey's High-Church party.

The proper business of the Museum was taken to be the study of the Universe in a National University; of Nature in its Unity, and in its several component parts, in its history, in its relation to her Maker and to Man – the words are Acland's, and the vision was taken very seriously indeed: Astronomy, Geometry, Experimental Physics, Chemistry, Mineralogy, Geology, Zoology, Anatomy, Physiology, and Medicine were to be accommodated.

It fell to John Ruskin, Acland's friend, to translate into a building the grand design of housing lecture rooms, laboratories, and a museum of natural history under a single roof, and he did so with his usual energy and enthusiasm. Gothic, of course, ostensibly Italianate (Ruskin had published his *Stones of Venice* in 1851–3) to a design by Benjamin Woodward, the Dublin architect – who did not live to see the building occupied. It is an immense, more or less square, building, with an open central court covered with a glass roof, and a gallery all round forming an ambulatory from which rooms open off; the gallery supported by stone piers with exquisitely cut foliage capitals, the glass roof – three steeply pitched 'naves' with lower 'aisles' between – carried on groups of soaring cast-iron columns with magnificent wrought-iron decoration in the spandrels. Thus far art, symbolizing in this temple of the sciences, the new light, and new aspirations.

But Ruskin's passion could not be contained by a merely symbolic mode. The Museum had, in the eyes of its promoters, not only a scientific but a broadly educational, even a moral, purpose – to give material form to 'the Art of the Great Artificer', and hence it was decided in the decoration of the Museum 'to employ so much of system as to make the ornamental parts of the fabric *really*, and *obviously useful*, as a part of the exhibition of natural objects'.

Thus the polished stone shafts which carry the gallery illustrate 'British Rocks'. The lower arcade on the west side going north displays six examples of granite; the northernmost one, for example, is a shaft of red granite of Ross and Mull (the gift of the Duke of Argyll) surmounted by a sculptured capital of liliaceous plants – lilium, tulipa, fritillaria, with adjacent corbels representing yucca and aloe. In the spandrels of the ironwork the flower and fruit of lime, chestnut, sycamore, walnut, palm, and other trees are represented, and in the capitals and elsewhere leaves of elm, briar, water-lily, passion-flower, ivy, holly, and many others. The upper windows of the front illustrate flora and fauna, those to the south vertebrates. It was a splendid scheme but it ran out of steam and out of money and the sculptured programme was never completed, most of the ground-floor windows remaining uncut.

Only Ruskin could have conceived it and only he could have disowned it. (Twenty years later he resigned and withdrew from the University as a protest against the appointment of a vivisectionist to the Chair of Physiology.) Modern Science has long since moved elsewhere, but the original principles of the Museum and the original displays are not much modified. A fragment of marble pavement uncovered at Pompeii sits beside a model of the food web in Wytham Wood; and near by a blown-up three-dimensional model of the double helix of the DNA molecule stands. It is a monument, one in the creation of which, as Acland declared, 'Love of Art, Love of Nature, Love of Science, Love of working-men, in their several bearings, practical, poetical, heart-lifting, animated all concerned'.

UNIVERSITY
PARKS
3C

'A place for Recreation of youth,' remarked the estimable Dr Plot in his *Natural History of Oxfordshire* published in 1676, 'and where the pastimes of the scholars were solemnized', and still today that can stand as an

143

accurate enough description of the Parks.

In the Domesday survey of 1086 it appears that the land was part of 30 acres (12 hectares) held by Robert d'Oilly, the first Norman sheriff of Oxford and builder of the Castle; by 1864 when the University completed its purchase from Merton College, the Park, or Beaumont Fields as they were then known, had grown to nearly a hundred acres (40 hectares) – including the land now occupied by the Science Area, but not at that time extending to the east much beyond the University cricket ground. Subsequently it grew by purchase and gift to its present extent, stretching beyond the Cherwell as far as New Marston.

The west part, fronting on Parks Road, is given over to sporting activities of various kinds; it also affords the best views of Keble chapel and of the new Department of Engineering building, comfortably anchored to the north, with the fulfilled air of an ocean liner at its pier. East of the cricket ground a rough agricultural character develops and extends to the Cherwell and beyond. The best walks are along the river, especially on the far bank which is reached by a bridge east of the cricket pavilion – north to the Victoria Arms, south to Magdalen and St Catherine's and St Clement's, east by narrow lanes to New Marston.

The Parks are notable for their splendid trees and shrubs, both indigenous and exotic. The fine stock of elms suffered greatly from the rampant Dutch elm disease of 1975–8 and it left aching gaps; losses included the magnificent stands near the Lady Margaret gate and near South Lodge (at the junction of South Parks Road and St Cross Road) which probably dated from the Restoration replanting of elms cut down to build defences during the Civil War.

The flower gardening is indifferent although there is one display worth a special visit on a July day: a crescent and rather surreptitious bed by the South Lodge gate, crammed with geraniums, begonia, nasturtiums, sweet peas, carnations, dahlias, daisies, antirrhinums, marigolds, phlox, chrysanthemums, and overburdened fuchsia. It is a display of the most resplendent vulgarity which looks as if it were the work of a deranged and colour-blind botanist.

UNIVERSITY SPORTS CENTRE
8E

For the historically minded, here on this windy track in 1954 the first sub four-minute mile was run by Roger Bannister of Exeter College. Since much developed, with the addition of a modern stand and field-house.

WADHAM COLLEGE
5C

It would be nice to say that Wadham's set-back from Parks Road is a relaxing thing, but the twin aprons of lawn with neither flower nor shrub for relief serve to make an already severe front implacable. Severity here means symmetry and uniformity – windows, gables, moulding, chimneys, battlements – and combined with the smoothness of the restored stone it is exceedingly daunting.

The Front Quad is no easier on the eye; it is a neatly carved stone box that one needs no encouragement to escape from. Interiors on the east side, opposite the gate-tower, are hall and chapel. The hall has the grandest roof of any college hall, technically a hammerbeam, steeply pitched, and alive with a cascade of posts, struts, beams, braces, and pendants. The chapel has a delicate screen with exquisitely elaborate filigree carving and decorative openwork cresting.

All this – front and quadrangle – is part of the original building of 1610–13 and it shows what can be achieved in a short time with a careful design purposefully executed. And there is no doubt that a few more purposeful designs like it would have made Oxford visually a much less interesting place than it is.

But Wadham compensates elsewhere. In the Back Quad for a start – i.e. the quad contained in the angle of Holywell and Parks Road, marked by the Kings Arms on the outside. To the right a large solid-looking late seventeenth-century house; facing it a building unmistakably Oxford *c*.1935 but really 1951–4 and the last anaemic hurrah of the style that began with the Radcliffe Science Library twenty years earlier. Between the two, bounded by the Kings Arms on the west end and the Holywell Music Room on the east, the shambling backs of the seventeenth-century houses and shops which face on to Holywell Street.

It would have been easy to have left the cheerful confusion of chimneys, roofs, and windows to exercise their natural charm. But someone at Wadham has a taste for adventure. Built in front of the houses is a large, raised terrace approached by a measured flight of cobbled steps. It is only at the top that the point of it becomes clear. Inset, the terrace has two deep wells surrounded by coping (cleverly designed to make sitting impossible). The smaller provides light for the basement of Blackwell's Music Shop on Holywell Street. The other is a severe oblong court with large lead-encased windows, utterly private and impregnable. Above Blackwell's a projecting range of college rooms looks from the terrace right into the heads of the trees in the quadrangle below.

It all seems simply imaginative rather than necessary but it is as good in its way as Brasenose's famous infill and beyond comparison better than Blackwell's earlier collaboration with Trinity at their main shop. It is the sort of thing that architectural prizes are invented for. The architects are Gillespie, Kidd and Coia.

That dates from 1971–2 and Gillespie, Kidd and Coia did it again in 1975–7 when they were hired to design a building to combine a new library and residential sets. Square in outline, mountainous in its proportions, in coarsely shuttered yellow concrete it lies beyond the entrance quadrangle to the east, abutting Savile Road, and its location is the only discreet thing about it. It is reached from the Back Quad up a broad gentle staircase (Wadham adopts a Fabian approach to its surprises) across the outside of the east end of the hall and along a raised walkway at the level at which the library is entered. So a terrace again. On to the terrace lets an immense dark glass window which rises through two and a half storeys to illuminate an entrance well set in the south-west corner of the library, and

on the same side over the residential part an area of prominent mansard roofing in harsh, ribbed lead. So a well and lead again. But it is like Hyde to Holywell Court's Jekyll, and not adventurous but downright risky. Brutalism squared. Yet it is undoubtedly impressive; many will hate it.

By an accident of history Wadham may have acquired in its new library the last monument to the Pahlavi dynasty: it was built with a gift of £125,000 from the Iranian Imperial Foundation and is named after the late Shah of Iran's sister, Princess Ashraf.

In David Loggan's *Oxonia Illustrata* (1675) there is an engraving of Wadham garden, all pleached alleys, clipped yew, and geometrical patterns (long ago swept away) in the middle of which is a Mount with a statue of Hercules on top. In the garden beneath the new library is its jokey reincarnation – a statue (by John Doubleday) of Sir Maurice Bowra, Warden of Wadham 1938–70: powerfully modelled arms, chest, and head, but with neither abdomen nor legs, perched on a solid chair on a raised plinth in the shadow of a building he would surely have hated. It is to the college's credit that it refused to succumb to Oxford's tradition of polite memorialization.

But Wadham has always had clever men, and been attractive to independent spirits. Two great and idiosyncratic architects, T. G. Jackson who put his stamp on Oxford, and Christopher Wren who put his on England, got their education there. John Wilkins, Warden 1648–59, was shrewd enough to marry Oliver Cromwell's sister, to found the Royal Society, and to be given preferment by both the Commonwealth and Charles II. Wadham has nurtured John Wilmot the libertine Earl of Rochester and a poet most of whose poetry was unprintable, Sir Thomas Beecham the libertine conductor, Mr Michael Foot the libertarian politician, and Professor R. V. Jones who combined a role as one of the leaders in the brilliantly effective secret war waged by British Scientific Intelligence against the Nazis between 1939 and 1945 with a most formidable talent as a practical joker.

WALTON STREET
5B

It picks a rather uncertain way north from Worcester College, with only the Oxford University Press to relieve the drabness, until dispossessed by Kingston Road.

WALTON WELL ROAD
3A

Walton Street draining away into Port Meadow. A. E. Coppard (1878–1957), short-story writer and poet, worked at the Eagle Ironworks, which still dominates the locality.

WELLINGTON SQUARE
4B

Much redeveloped in recent years with the removal to it of the central administrative offices of the University. The University Chest in the north-east (Sir Leslie Martin, 1969–73) is sensible and businesslike, the University Graduate Building in the north fronted by a wide terrace has a cool, laid-back look. The yellow-brick terraced housing on the other sides remains. Access to Little Clarendon Street is now only pedestrian.

147

A suburban shopping plaza come to town, fashioned out of the decay o medieval and Victorian St Ebbe's. No doubt it has inhibited developmen elsewhere, and that is a service to a city that commerce has long threatenec but never managed to destroy; its blight is very widespread and only a fev pockets of the old St Ebbe's are left – the small group of seventeenth century houses on Turn Again Lane and St Ebbe's church, but not mucl else.

Methodist Teachers' Training College on a good hillside site west of th city, with views much spoiled by the Central Electricity Generating Board

Founded in 1965 on the far side of Oxford as Iffley College, its building completed in 1974, no other college can boast an adventure playground c washing lines with assorted underwear streaming in the breeze. Decorur scarcely admits the possibility, but Wolfson is assured enough to get awa with that and much else.

Imagination helps (the combination of Powell and Moya as architec and Sir Isaiah Berlin and others of like mind as clients) and so does larg quantities of money (a total of nearly £3 million contributed by Isaa Wolfson and the Ford Foundation) and together they translate into a ver distinctive and stylish achievement. What is original is the idea of residential college for graduates of both sexes designed to make possible true twentieth-century egalitarian collegiality, recognizing families an children as an appropriate and enlivening addition to the texture college life.

All this is material in the architecture which makes the most of a fine si on the west bank of the Cherwell in north Oxford (next the Cherwe Boathouse). The main quadrangle is open to the east and steps down fro terraced lawn to a pool with navigable access to the river, turning it intc punt dock in the summer. It is a light and relaxing space enclosed by thre and four-storeyed wings, partly academic in use, partly domestic, and tl external galleries and open terraces give it an air of easy sociability. bow-like bridge over the Cherwell leads to the water meadows and willo lined river walks on the east bank. To the north a small, gloomy quadrang with too many trees, no doubt an attempt to screen the garage blo beyond. Hall, library, and other offices occupy a small quad to the west.

Buildings follow the different levels of the site and this makes for mu variation in height but any threatening casualness is disciplined by t strong horizontal members which pull everything together; they in th turn are offset by the powerful rhythm of the supporting concrete pill throughout, with a resulting arcade effect which is very pleasing. T emphasis is on surfaces and their relationship and careful attention l been given to textures: concrete, red stock bricks, granite setts, whi painted cement blocks, glass, grass, trees, water, and (prominent to t east) sky. There are no dramatic accents and no straining after novelty.] formal elements are widely prominent. Visible interiors are of studies a

1

sitting rooms, kitchens and laundries – all as unceremonial as it is possible to imagine.

WOLVERCOTE The industrial suburb of Godstow, it manages to accommodate an immense paper mill employing 700 people, and a village green, without any sense of strain. On the north edge of Port Meadow it has a good grassy bathing place, a good view of the Oxford skyline, and a touching memorial to two Royal Flying Corps officers who, flying in 1912 from a temporary airfield in Port Meadow, 'met their deaths in the wreck of a monoplane'.

WOODSTOCK ROAD It still retains some of the spacious style that the Banbury Road has sacrificed to private hotels, banks, garages, and the retail trade, and offers the only pleasing entrance to Oxford. It maintains its character to the very edge of the city centre, with its large red-brick houses well set back behind screens of flowering shrubs and trees. Number 300 has fragments of medieval arches (late twelfth century) in the garden, perhaps from Beaumont Palace, a royal residence once on the site of Gloucester Green.

WORCESTER COLLEGE
5B
Until the opening up of Beaumont Street in 1828 Worcester was geographically remote, and even after that still something of a joke: 'Botany Bay' was its nineteenth-century nickname. It started life as a college for Benedictine monks of the southern province, run on a co-operative principle – expenses were levied on the Benedictine houses which sent students and the abbeys themselves maintained lodgings (*camerae* or *mansiones*) for their own monks.

That was Gloucester College (named from an earlier house of study maintained by Gloucester Abbey which the college absorbed) and it was already in existence by the end of the thirteenth century. It was dissolved in 1541 and for a century and a half it survived precariously as Gloucester Hall; so precariously that it was a candidate to become in turn the episcopal palace of the new diocese of Oxford, the site of St John's College, the site of Wadham College, and a college for Greek Orthodox clergy, as well as being the residence for sixty-two years of Thomas Allen the Elizabethan astrologer and mathematician – and by common repute a magician (his servant used to say that 'he met the spirits coming up the stairs like bees').

The result of this disturbed and indeterminate interlude was that when Sir Thomas Cookes refounded the Hall as Worcester College (he was a Worcestershire man) in 1714 the buildings of the monastic college remained, although in a very dilapidated state, and the *camerae* have (largely by accident since the original plans called for their demolition) survived. One range – that on the south side of the quadrangle – is more or less intact, and framed as they are by an eighteenth-century classical composition they have a very agreeable cottage-like intimacy. In comparison the eighteenth-century buildings in the entrance block – chapel, hall, library over, with a spacious open colonnade to the quadrangle – and the north range of 19 bays and 3 storeys opposite the

Worcester College, backs of the *camerae*

camerae (all to a design by Dr George Clarke of All Souls, which he apparently discussed with Hawksmoor) seem very assertive, an effect much exaggerated by the lie of the land which sets the newer buildings atop high embankments overlooking a 'sunken' lawn. The Provost's house (Henry Keene, 1773–6) stands at the end of the north range overlooking its own garden; it is patrician and therefore not at all assertive.

The back of the *camerae* is a model of romantic confusion: coarse rubble and dressed stone, trefoil windows with barge-boards, stone hood-moulds gables and chimneys, stone slate roofs in projecting, receding, and intersecting planes, all hung with wisteria and climbed by roses and ivy This faces the garden and modern buildings of 1939, 1961, and 1971. It is customary to overrate the garden itself. It is notable for its trees incorporates a cricket ground, and, in the words of an early guide-book, 'i embellished with a large sheet of artificial water, well stocked with fish'.

The history of Worcester is a story of fits and starts. The most singular fa is without question the work of William Burges who redid James Wyatt'

Opposite: Security at Worcester College

chapel interior (1783) in 1863–4. The chapel's muddy light cannot conceal – nor does it subdue – the extraordinary inventiveness and profusion of Burges's decorative scheme which has as its excuse the illustration of the *Benedicite* and the *Te Deum* – man and nature uniting in worship of their maker. The panelled frescoes on the walls teem with plants, foliage, animals, and birds and the same motifs are carried over to the carving and inlay of the stalls and to the rich stucco ceiling. A figure frieze and a disjointed inscription (from the *Te Deum*) encircles the room beneath the windows; statues of the evangelists fill corner niches; and saints and doctors are depicted (in antique Roman style) in the mosaic of the floor. A picture of the Entombment over the altar is flanked by a Benedictine presenting a model of Gloucester College and by Sir Thomas Cookes presenting a model of Worcester. An exquisite alabaster lectern (by W. G. Nicholl) with matching candlesticks takes away what breath is left.

In 1877 Burges also redid Wyatt's decoration of the hall and addressed it with the same desperate energy; in 1964, finding it too strong for their taste, the college re-Wyattized it.

WYCLIFFE COLLEGE
3C

To the passer-by distracted by the confusion of traffic on the Banbury Road–Norham Gardens junction at which it stands, not very obviously a collegiate group, but in fact an Anglican theological college of evangelical leanings.

WYTHAM

An unspoiled stone-and-thatch village once famous for its strawberry beds in the shadow of Wytham Hill, site of the University Field Station. Wytham Abbey is a former seat of the Earls of Abingdon. The church has memorial to the brother of Henry Purcell the composer.

ZOOLOGY AND PSYCHOLOGY BUILDING
4D

A concrete corner-stopper at South Parks Road and St Cross Road (1965–70), receding in a series of gigantic steps on the inside, but nothing to help it facing the other way. There is a point at which physical size can cause the imagination to falter and it may be that in this building Sir Leslie Martin has passed it.

Index

Abingdon, Earls of, *see* Wytham
Abingdon Grammar School, *see*
Pembroke College
Abingdon, Mayor and Corporation, *see*
Pembroke College
Acland, Henry, *see* University Museum
Adoration of the Magi, *see* Exeter College
Agriculture, Institute of, *see* Parks Road
Ahrends, Burton and Koralek, *see* Keble
College
Aldrich, Henry, *see* Christ Church
Alexander I, Emperor of Russia, *see*
Merton College
Alfred, King, *see* Gloucester Green,
Merton College, University College
Alice in Wonderland, *see* Christ Church,
Osney
Allen, Thomas, *see* Worcester College
Amis, Kingsley, *see* St John's College
Ampleforth, abbey, *see* St Benet's Hall
Anatomy of Melancholie, *see* St Thomas
the Martyr
Angel (former inn), *see* Angel and
Greyhound Meadows
Anglo-Saxon Chronicle, *see* North
Hinksey
Anglo-Saxon Oxford, *see* New Inn Hall
Street, St Aldate's, St Michael-at-the-
North-Gate
Anne, Queen, *see* Radcliffe Camera,
University College
Annora (anchoress), see Iffley
Antoinette, Marie, *see* St Hugh's College
Apollo, Temple of, *see* Ashmolean
Museum
Architects Co-Partnership, *see* St John's
College
Architecture, Five Orders of, *see*
Bodleian Library
Argyll, Duke of, *see* University Museum
Aristotle's Well, *see* Aristotle Lane
Arlosh Hall, *see* Manchester College
Arts and Sciences at Trinity College 1977,
see Trinity College
Arundel marbles, *see* Old Ashmolean
Arup Associates, *see* St John's College,
Somerville College
Ashmole, Elias, *see* Ashmolean Museum,
Old Ashmolean, Pitt Rivers Museum
Asquith, H. J., *see* Oxford Union
Society
Aubrey, John, *see* Cornmarket, St Mary
Magdalen
Auden, W. H., *see* Christ Church
Augustinian Canons (former houses), *see*
Brasenose College, Christ Church,
New Inn Hall Street, Osney
Austin Friars, *see* Merton College

Bacon, Roger, *see* Folly Bridge
Baker, Herbert, *see* Rhodes House
Balliol–St Anne's Graduate Residence,
see Law Library

Bannister, Roger, *see* University Sports
Centre
Barberini, Piazza, *see* Radcliffe Infirmary
Baring, Thomas, *see* Hertford College
Basevi, G., *see* Balliol College
Bathurst, Ralph, *see* St John's College
Bear Lane Gallery, *see* Bear Lane
Beaumont Fields, *see* University Parks
Beaumont Palace, *see* Gloucester Green,
St John's College, Woodstock Road
Becket Street, *see* St Thomas the Martyr
Beecham, Sir Thomas, *see* Wadham
College
Beef Lane, *see* Pembroke College
'Beehives', *see* St John's College
Beerbohm, Max, *see* Randolph Hotel,
Sheldonian Theatre
Belsyre Court, *see* Observatory Street
Benedictines (former houses), *see*
Durham College, Godstow, Worcester
College
Benedictines of Ampleforth, *see* St
Benet's Hall
Berlin, Isaiah, *see* Wolfson College
Bernini, Giovanni, *see* Radcliffe
Infirmary
Besse, Antonin, *see* St Antony's College
Betjeman, John, *see* All Souls College,
Balliol College, St Barnabas
Bird, Francis, *see* University College
Black Bourton, *see* Town Hall
Blackfriars, *see* Merton College
Black Hall, *see* Queen Elizabeth House
Blackwell, B. H., *see* St Clement's
Blackwell's, *see* Hythe Bridge Street,
Trinity College, Wadham College
Blomfield, Arthur, *see* Jericho, Radcliffe
Infirmary, St Barnabas
Bocardo, prison, *see* St Michael-at-the-
North-Gate
Bodley, G. F., *see* Examination Schools,
St John Evangelist, University College
Bodley, Sir Thomas, *see* Bodleian Lib-
rary, Merton College
Bodley and Garner, *see* Christ Church,
Magdalen College
Bone hole, *see* St Aldate
'Botany Bay', *see* Worcester College
Bowra, Maurice, *see* Wadham College
Brass Rubbing Centre, *see* St Mary the
Virgin
Breakspear, Nicolas (Pope Hadrian IV),
see Binsey
Breyne, André de, *see* Keble College
'Bridge of Sighs', *see* Hertford College
British Council, *see* Beaumont Buildings
Broadgates Hall, *see* Pembroke College
Brome, Adam de, *see* Oriel College, St
Mary the Virgin
Brown, Capability, *see* St John's College
Buckler, J. C., *see* Magdalen College
Burges, William, *see* Worcester College
Burne-Jones, Edward, *see* Christ Church,

Exeter College, Lady Margaret Hall,
Manchester College, Oxford Union
Society, St Edmund Hall
Burton, Robert, *see* St Thomas the
Martyr
Bus Station, *see* Gloucester Green
Butterfield, William, *see* Balliol College,
Keble College, Merton College

'Cain and Abel', *see* Brasenose College
Camerae, *see* Worcester College
Campion, Edmund, *see* St John's College
Cardinal College, *see* Christ Church
Carlingford, Lord, *see* Examination
Schools
Carlyle, Thomas, *see* Keble College
Carmelite Friars, *see* Gloucester Green,
Merton College
Caroline, Queen, *see* The Queen's College
Carroll, Lewis (C.L. Dodgson), *see* Christ
Church, Old Ashmolean, Osney, St
Aldate's
'Caudwell's Castle', *see* Folly Bridge
Cézanne, Paul, *see* Ashmolean Museum
Champneys, Basil, *see* Examination
Schools, Indian Institute, Linacre
College, Mansfield College, Merton
College, Oriel College, St Peter's
College, Somerville College
Chancellor's Court, *see* St Mary the
Virgin
Channon, Henry, *see* Ashmolean
Museum
Chantrey, Francis, *see* Christ Church
Charles I, King, *see* The Queen's College,
St John's College
Charles II, King, *see* Wadham College
Charles Street, *see* Turn Again Lane
Charlotte, Queen, *see* The Queen's
College
Chaucer, Geoffrey, *see* Osney
Chavasse, F. J., *see* St Peter's College
Chavasse, Noel, *see* St Peter's College
Cherwell Edge, *see* Linacre College
Chichele, Henry, *see* All Souls College
Cistercians (former houses), *see* Rewley
Abbey, St Bernard's College
Clarendon, Earl of (Edward Hyde), *see*
Clarendon Building
Clarendon Hotel (former), *see* Corn-
market
Clarke, George, *see* Christ Church,
Worcester College
Cockerell, C. R., *see* Ashmolean Museum
Codrington Library, *see* All Souls College
Combe, Thomas, *see* Radcliffe Infirmary,
St Barnabas
Commonwealth Studies, Institute of, *see*
Queen Elizabeth House
Comper, Ninian, *see* Pusey House
Congregation House, *see* St Mary the
Virgin
Cook, Captain, *see* Pitt Rivers Museum

Cookes, Sir Thomas, *see* Worcester College

Cooper, Mrs Frank, *see* Angel and Greyhound Meadows

Coppard, A. E., *see* Walton Well Road

Cornwall, Edmund, Earl of, *see* Rewley Abbey

Corot, Jean Baptiste, *see* Ashmolean Museum

Cosimo, Piero di, *see* Ashmolean Museum

Cottingham, L., *see* Magdalen College

Courbet, Gustave, *see* Ashmolean Museum

Cowley Fathers, *see* St John Evangelist

Cowley St John, *see* Cowley

Cranmer, Thomas, *see* Broad Street, Martyrs' Memorial, St Mary the Virgin

Crew, Nathaniel, *see* Lincoln College

Croidon, John, *see* Carfax

Cromwell, Oliver, *see* Wadham College

Crosfield, Thomas, *see* The Queen's College

Crown Inn (former), *see* Cornmarket

Cumnor Hill, *see* St Philip and St James

DNA molecule, *see* University Museum

Dalwood, Hubert, *see* Nuffield College

Danby, Earl (Henry Danvers), *see* Botanic Garden

Deane, Thomas, *see* Examination Schools

Deane and Woodward, *see* St Hilda's College

Deirdre, *see* Oxford Girls' High School

d'Oilly, Robert, *see* Castle, University Parks

Domesday, *see* University Parks

Donne, John, *see* Hertford College

Doubleday, John, *see* Wadham College

Dowson, Philip, *see* Somerville College

Durham College (former), *see* Trinity College

Eagle Ironworks, *see* Walton Well Road

Educational Studies, Department of, *see* Norham Gardens

Edward, King of the West Saxons, *see* North Hinksey

Edward I, King, *see* Martyrs' Memorial

Edward III, King, *see* The Queen's College, St Bartholomew's Chapel

Edward IV, King, *see* Magdalen College

Edward VI, King, *see* All Souls College, Christ Church

Edward VII, King, *see* New Inn Hall Street

Eglesfield, Robert de, *see* The Queen's College

Einstein, Albert, *see* St Catherine's College

Eleanor's Cross (Waltham), *see* Martyrs' Memorial

Elizabeth I, Queen, *see* Bodleian Library, Jesus College, The Queen's College

Encaenia ('the Act'), *see* St Mary the Virgin, Sheldonian Theatre

English Faculty Library, *see* Law Library

Epstein, Jacob, *see* New College, Oxford

Girls' High School, St Catherine's College

Erasmus, Desiderius, *see* Corpus Christi College, New Inn Hall Street

'Erotic female figure', *see* St Michael-at-the-North-Gate

Evelyn, John, *see* All Souls College, Old Ashmolean

Fell, John, *see* Broad Walk

Ferry Hinksey, *see* Castle Street, Corpus Christi College, Folly Bridge, North Hinksey

Flaxman, John, *see* University College

Flore, *see* Maison Française

Florey Building, *see* St Clement's

Foot, Michael, *see* Wadham College

Ford, Onslow, *see* University College

Fornication Lane, *see* Brasenose Lane

Fortescue, Chicester Samuel Parkinson, *see* Examination Schools

Fox, Richard, *see* Corpus Christi College

Frewin Hall, *see* New Inn Hall Street

Friar Bacon's Study, *see* Folly Bridge

Fry, Margaret, *see* Somerville College

Fryman, John, *see* Beaumont Buildings, University College

Fuller, Isaac, *see* All Souls College, Magdalen College

Gates (city), *see* Town Wall

Gee's greenhouse, *see* North Parade

George II, King, *see* The Queen's College

George III, King, *see* The Queen's College

George IV, King, *see* Holywell Music Room

George Café, *see* George Street

Georgia, *see* Lincoln College

Gibbs, James, *see* All Souls College, Radcliffe Camera

Gill, Eric, *see* Binsey, Blackfriars, New College, Playhouse

Gillespie, Kidd and Coia, *see* Wadham College

Gladstone, W. E., *see* Oxford Union Society

Glazier, Thomas, *see* New College

Gloucester Abbey, *see* Worcester College

Gloucester College (former), *see* Worcester College

Gloucester Hall (former), *see* Worcester College

Godstow, *see* Wolvercote

Grand Pont, *see* Abingdon Road, Folly Bridge

Graves, Robert, *see* St John's College

Great Tom, *see* Osney

Greek Orthodox clergy, *see* Worcester College

Green, Dr Cecil, *see* Green College

Greyfriars, *see* Merton College, Paradise Square

Greyhound (former inn), *see* Angel and Greyhound Meadows

Grope Lane (former), *see* Magpie Lane

Guise, General John, *see* Christ Church

'Gunfield', *see* Norham Gardens

Gwynn, John, *see* Magdalen Bridge, Market

Halley, Edmund, *see* Queen's Lane

Handel, G. F., *see* Ashmolean Museum

Hansom, Joseph Aloysius, *see* St Aloysius

Hardy, Thomas, *see* Jericho

Hare, H. T., *see* St Clement's, Town Hall

Hart Hall (former), *see* Hertford College

Hastings, Lady Elizabeth, *see* The Queen's College

Hawksmoor, Nicholas, *see* All Souls College, Clarendon Building, Magdalen College, The Queen's College, Worcester College

Hayward, Sir Charles, *see* Keble College

Hayward, J., *see* Pembroke College

Heath, Edward, *see* Oxford Union Society

Henrietta Maria, Queen, *see* The Queen's College, St John's College

Henry I, King, *see* Gloucester Green

Henry II, King *see* Godstow

Henry VII, King, *see* Corpus Christi College

Henry VIII, King, *see* Christ Church, Osney

Hepworth, Barbara, *see* St Catherine's College

Hercules, *see* Wadham College

Hertford, Elias, *see* Hertford College

High School for Boys, *see* George Street

Hinksey Hill, *see* Abingdon Road, Folly Bridge

History Faculty Library, *see* Indian Institute

History of the Rebellion and Civil Wars in England, *see* Clarendon Building

Hitler, Adolf, *see* Rhodes House

Holford, Lord, *see* Cornmarket

Hopkins, Gerard Manley, *see* Binsey, St Aloysius, St Philip and St James

Housman, A. E., *see* Bodleian Library, St John's College

Humfrey, Duke of Gloucester, *see* Bodleian Library

Hunt, W. Holman, *see* Keble College, St Barnabas

Iffley College (former), *see* Wolfson College

Inchbold, John William, *see* Ashmolean Museum

Ipswich, *see* Christ Church

Iran, Shah of (late), *see* Wadham College

Isis House, *see* Folly Bridge

Jackson, Cyril, *see* Christ Church

Jackson, T. G., *see* Brasenose College, Examination Schools, George Street, Hertford College, Lincoln College, Queen's Lane, Radcliffe Science Library, Trinity College, Wadham College

Jacobsen, Arne, *see* The Queen's College, St Catherine's College

ames I, King, *see* Bodleian Library, Pembroke College
ames II, King, *see* University College
eune, Francis, *see* Pembroke College
eune, Margaret, *see* Pembroke College
ewish cemetery, *see* Botanic Garden, Synagogue
ewry, Great or King's, *see* Synagogue
ohn Rylands Library, *see* Indian Institute
ohnson, Samuel (Dr), *see* Pembroke College, Trinity College
ones, R. V., *see* Wadham College
owett, Benjamin, *see* Balliol College
ude the Obscure, *see* Jericho

eble, John, *see* Keble College
eene, Henry, *see* Balliol College, Radcliffe Observatory, Worcester College
ent, William, *see* St John's College
ettell, Hall, *see* Trinity College
ing, Robert, *see* Old Palace
irby Hall (Northants), *see* Examination Schools
ratzer, Nicholas, *see* Corpus Christi College

ancaster, Osbert, *see* Randolph Hotel
andor, Walter Savage, *see* St John's College
atimer, Hugh, *see* Broad Street, St Michael-at-the-North-Gate
aud, William, *see* Brasenose College, St John's College
awrence, T. E., *see* George Street
azarus, *see* New College
eopold, Prince, *see* Oxford University Appointments Committee
iddell, Alice, *see* Osney
iddell, Edith, *see* Christ Church
ight of the World, *see* Keble College, St Barnabas
utyens, Edwin, *see* Campion Hall

acmillan, Harold, *see* Oxford Union Society
acNeice, Louis, *see* St Clement's
agdalen Hall (former), *see* Hertford College
aillol, Aristide, *see* Maison Française
artin, Sir Leslie, *see* Law Library, Pembroke College, Wellington Square, Zoology and Psychology Building
artyr, Peter, *see* Christ Church
ary, Queen, *see* University College
ary Tudor, Queen, *see* St John's College
atilda, Empress, *see* Castle
erle, William, *see* Merton College
erton, Walter de, *see* Merton College
ethodism, *see* Lincoln College, New Inn Hall Street
ethodist Teachers' Training College, *see* Westminster College
icklem Hall (former), *see* Campion Hall
ilner, Alfred, *see* Corpus Christi College

Min, *see* Ashmolean Museum
Moberly, Charlotte, *see* St Hugh's College
More, Sir Thomas, *see* Corpus Christi College
Morris, Marshall & Faulkner, *see* Littlemore
Morris, William, 12; *see also* Exeter College, Littlemore, Magdalen College, Manchester College, Oxford Union Society, St Barnabas, St Edmund Hall
Morte d'Arthur, *see* Oxford Union Society
Murdoch, Iris, *see* Somerville College
Museum of the History of Science, *see* Old Ashmolean

Nash, John, *see* Magdalen College
Nelmes (Essex), *see* Balliol College
New Inn Hall (former), *see* St Peter's College New College - 86
Newman, John Henry, *see* Littlemore, St Mary the Virgin, Trinity College
Newport, Captain Christopher, *see* Ashmolean Museum
New Road Baptist Church, *see* Bonn Square
Newton, Richard, *see* Hertford College
Nicholl, W. G., *see* Ashmolean Museum, Worcester College
Nuclear Physics Laboratory, *see* Keble College
Nuffield, Lord, *see* Nuffield College
Nuns' Garden, *see* The Queen's College

Old Sheep Shop, *see* St Aldate's
Orchard, William, *see* Christ Church
Osney Abbey, *see* Cowley, St Thomas the Martyr
'Ox ford', *see* Castle Street, North Hinksey
Oxford Canal Company, *see* Nuffield College, Oxford Canal, St Peter's College
Oxford English Dictionary, *see* Old Ashmolean
Oxford Movement, *see* Keble College
Oxford Preservation Trust, *see* Roger Bacon Lane
Oxford University Students Union, *see* Oxford Union Society

Pahlavi, Princess Ashraf, *see* Wadham College
Palmer, Samuel, *see* Ashmolean Museum
Park Lodge, *see* Parks Road
Pater, Walter, *see* Brasenose College
Pembroke, Earl of (William Herbert), *see* Bodleian Library, Pembroke College
Penicillin, *see* Botanic Garden, Old Ashmolean
Pevsner, Nikolaus, *see* Christ Church, Oxford University Appointments Committee, Radcliffe Camera, Radcliffe Observatory, St Peter-in-the-East
Philippa, Queen, *see* The Queen's College

Pierce, Edward, *see* Ashmolean Museum
Piper, John, *see* Nuffield College
Pissarro, Camille, *see* Ashmolean Museum
Pitt Rivers, Augustus, *see* Pitt Rivers Museum
Pompeii, *see* University Museum
Pope, Sir Thomas, *see* St John's College, Trinity College
Port Meadow, *see* Aristotle Lane
Postmaster's Hall, *see* Merton Street
Powell & Moya, *see* Blue Boar Street, Brasenose College, Christ Church, Wolfson College
Powhatan, *see* Ashmolean Museum
Price, Hugh, *see* Jesus College
Prideaux, Humphrey, *see* Balliol College
Prison, Oxford, *see* Castle
Pugin, A. W. N., *see* Magdalen College
Purcell, Henry, *see* Wytham
Pusey, Edward Bouverie, *see* Pusey House, University Museum

Quatermaine's Stables (Lincoln College), *see* Bear Lane

Radcliffe, John, *see* Lincoln College, Radcliffe Camera, Radcliffe Infirmary, University College
Radcliffe College (former), *see* Green College
Rathbone, Eleanor, *see* Somerville College
Repton, Humphry, *see* Magdalen College, St John's College
Reynolds, Sir Joshua, *see* New College
Reyntiens, Patrick, *see* Nuffield College
Rhodes, Cecil, *see* King Edward Street, Oriel College, Rhodes House
Richard I, King, *see* Gloucester Green
Richard III, King, *see* Magdalen College
Richards, Ceri, *see* Edmund Hall
Richardson, Albert, *see* St Hilda's College
Ridley, Nicholas, *see* Broad Street, Martyrs' Memorial, St Michael-at-the-North-Gate
Roberts, David, *see* Longwall Street, St Hugh's College
Rochester, Earl of (John Wilmot), *see* Wadham College
Rosamond, Fair, *see* Godstow
Rossetti, Dante Gabriel, *see* Oxford Union Society
Roubiliac, Louis François, *see* Ashmolean Museum
Royal Society, *see* Wadham College
Rusk, Dean, *see* St John's College
Ruskin, John, *see* Corpus Christi College, Folly Bridge, Keble College, North Hinksey, University Museum

St Alban Hall (former), *see* Merton College
St Andrew, church (Headington), *see* Old Headington
St Bartholomew, relics, *see* St Bartholomew's Chapel

St Bernard's College (former), *see* St John's College

St Columba, church, *see* Alfred Street

St Edmund and St Frideswide, church (Iffley Road), *see* Greyfriars

St Edmund of Abingdon, *see* St Edmund Hall

St Felix, relics, *see* St Aloysius

St Francis of Assisi, relics, *see* St Aloysius

St Frideswide, *see* Binsey, Christ Church

St Frideswide (Augustinian Priory), *see* Christ Church, Merton College, Osney, The Queen's College, St Aldate's

St Frideswide, church (Botley Road), *see* Osney

St George's Chapel, *see* Castle

St Giles' House, *see* St Giles'

St James, church (Beauchamp Lane), *see* Cowley

St John the Baptist (former church), *see* Merton College

St John the Baptist (former hospital), *see* Magdalen College

St Margaret of Antioch, church (Binsey), *see* Binsey

St Martin (former church), *see* Carfax, St Clement

St Mary and St Nicholas, church (Littlemore), *see* Littlemore

St Mary's College (former), *see* Brasenose College, New Inn Hall Street

St Mary's Hall (former), *see* Oriel College

St Nicholas, church (Old Marston), *see* Marston Village

St Peter-le-Bailey (former church), *see* St Peter's College

St Scholastica, feast, *see* Carfax

St Theodore, relics, *see* St Aloysius

Sainte Chapelle, *see* Exeter College

Salisbury, Lord, *see* Oxford Union Society

Salvin, Anthony, *see* Balliol College

'Samson killing a Philistine', *see* Brasenose College

Savile, Sir Henry, *see* Merton College

Sayers, Dorothy, *see* Somerville College

Scott, George Gilbert, *see* Exeter College, New College, St Mary Magdalen, University College

Scott, George Gilbert, the younger, *see* St John's College

Scott, Giles Gilbert, *see* Lady Margaret Hall, Magdalen College, St Anne's College

Scott, John (Lord Eldon), *see* University College

Scott, William (Lord Stowell), *see* University College

Shakespeare, William, *see* Cornmarket

Sheldon, Gilbert, *see* Sheldonian Theatre

Shelley, Percy Bysshe, *see* University College

Sibthorp, John, *see* St Hilda's College

Smith, William, *see* Lincoln College

Smithson, Alison and Peter, *see* St Hilda's College

Society of Jesus, *see* Campion Hall, St Aloysius

Society of Oxford Home Students, *see* St Anne's College

Society of St John Evangelist, *see* St John Evangelist

South Lodge, *see* University Parks

Speedwell Street, *see* St Aldate's

Stanier, Maida, *see* Park Town

Stationers' Company, *see* Bodleian Library

Statistics, Institute of, *see* Law Library

Steele, Richard, *see* The Queen's College

Stephen, King, *see* Castle

Stirling, James, *see* St Clement's

Stone, Nicholas, *see* Botanic Garden, St Mary the Virgin

Stone's Almshouses, *see* St Clement's

Stones of Venice, *see* University Museum

Stradivarius, *see* Ashmolean Museum

Streater, Robert, *see* Sheldonian Theatre

Street, G. E., *see* St Philip and St James

Swyndolnestock tavern, *see* Carfax

Taylor, A. J. P., *see* Holywell Ford

Taylor, Sir Robert, *see* Ashmolean Museum

Temple Cowley, *see* Cowley

Tennis (Real, Royal, Court), *see* Oriel Street

Tesdale, Thomas, *see* Pembroke College

Thatcher, Margaret, *see* Somerville College

Thomas, Dylan, *see* Holywell Ford, St Clement's

Thornhill, Sir James, *see* All Souls College

Thorpe, Jeremy, *see* Oxford Union Society

Through the Looking Glass, *see* St Aldate's

Tissot, James Jacques Joseph, *see* Examination Schools

Townesend, William, *see* Magdalen College, Trinity College

Toynbee, Arnold, *see* Corpus Christi College

Trade Union Movement, *see* Ruskin College

Tradescant, John the Elder, *see* Ashmolean Museum, Pitt Rivers Museum

Tradescant, John the Younger, *see* Ashmolean Museum

Turner, William, 'of Oxford', *see* Town Hall

Unitarian Disserting Academy, *see* Manchester College

University Chest (administrative building), *see* Little Clarendon Street, Wellington Square

University Chest (medieval strongbox), *see* Ashmolean Museum

University Field Station, *see* Wytham

University Graduate Building, *see* Little Clarendon Street, Wellington Square

University picture gallery, *see* Ashmolean Museum

University Press, *see* Sheldonian Theatre

University Theatre, *see* Playhouse

van Linge, Abraham, *see* University College

van Linge, Bernard, *see* Lincoln College

Victoria, Queen, *see* Oxford University Appointments Committee, Town Hall

von Trott zu Solz, Adam, *see* Rhodes House

Vrooman, Walter, *see* Ruskin College

Wall paintings (Elizabethan), *see* Cornmarket

Ward, Barbara, *see* Somerville College

War Memorial Garden, *see* Trill Mill Stream

Warren, E. P., *see* Balliol College

Warton, Thomas, *see* Trinity College

Waterhouse, Alfred, *see* Balliol College

Waugh, Evelyn, *see* Hertford College

Wesley, John, *see* Christ Church, Lincoln College, New Inn Hall Street

Wesley Memorial Church, *see* St Michael's Street

White, Eirene, *see* Somerville College

White, Sir Thomas, *see* St John's College

Wilde, Oscar, *see* Corpus Christi College

Wilkins, John, *see* Wadham College

Wilkinson, William, *see* Randolph Hotel

William of Waynflete, *see* Magdalen College

William of Wykeham, *see* New College

Williams, Joseph, *see* Ashmolean Museum

Williams, Shirley, *see* Somerville College

Wilson, Colin St J., *see* Law Library

Winds, Tower of, *see* Radcliffe Observatory

Wolfson, Isaac, *see* Wolfson College

Wolsey, Thomas, *see* Christ Church

Wood, Anthony, *see* Angel and Greyhound Meadows, Magdalen College, Merton College, Merton Street, Mitre Hotel

Woodward, Benjamin, *see* Oxford Union Society, University Museum

Wordsworth, Elizabeth, *see* St Hugh's College

Workers' Educational Association, *see* Ruskin College

Worthington, Hubert, *see* Merton College, Radcliffe Science Library

Wren, Sir Christopher, *see* All Souls College, Ashmolean Museum, Christ Church, Divinity School, The Queen's College, Sheldonian Theatre, Trinity College, Wadham College

Wyatt, James, *see* Christ Church, Magdalen College, Oriel College, Radcliffe Observatory, Worcester College

Wytham Wood, *see* University Museum

Zuleika Dobson, *see* Randolph Hotel, Sheldonian Theatre

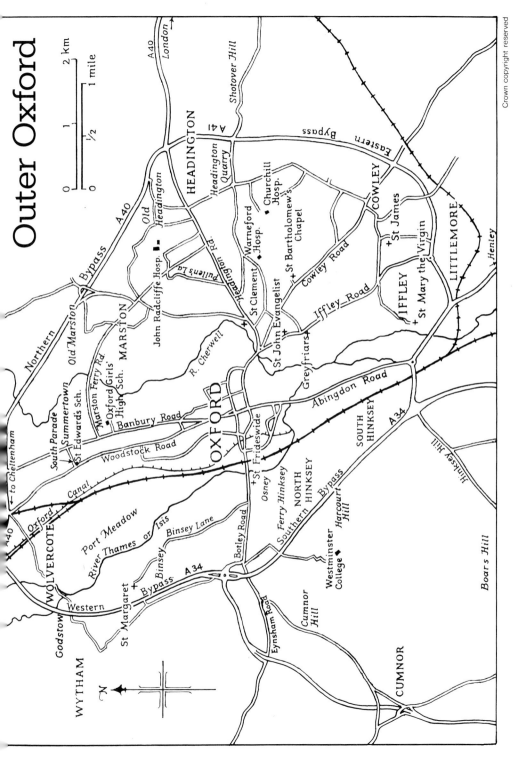

Outer Oxford

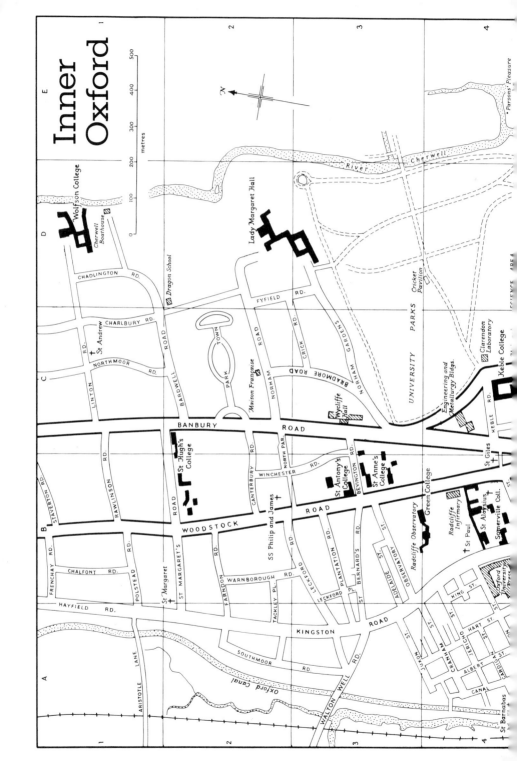

St Catherine's College
Low Library
Holywell Manor
St Cross College
Balliol-St Anne's Graduate Bldg.
MANOR RD.
Holywell Ford
Addison's Walk
The Paddock
Deer Park
The Grove
MILL LANE
Magdalen College
Magdalen College School
St Hilda's College
Rose Garden
Botanic Garden
Magdalen Bridge
Angel & Greyhound Meadows
Florey Bldg.
Wayfitter Bldg.
THE PLAIN
ST CLEMENTS
CowLEY RD.
COWLEY ROAD
IFFLEY ROAD
TYNDALE ST.
DAWSON ST.
CIRCUS
TEMPLE ST.
TEMPLE
MARION ST.
SOUTHMOOR ST.
St John St Evangelist
University Sports Centre

MANSFIELD ROAD
Mansfield College
New College School
Wadham College
Manchester Coll.
Music Room Coll.
Oriental Languages Inst.
JOWETT WALK
HOLYWELL STREET
New College
Old Town Wall
St Peter's in the East
St Edmund Hall
NEW COLLEGE LANE
QUEEN'S LANE
Queen's College
All Souls College
The Queen's College
HIGH STREET
LONGWALL ST.
Examination Schools
LOGIC LANE
MERTON College
MERTON STREET
ROSE LANE
MERTON FIELDS
MERTON WALK
Deadman's Walk
Broad Walk
New Walk
CHRIST CHURCH MEADOW

PARKS ROAD
ST CROSS ROAD
New Bodleian
Trinity College
Old Ashmolean
BROAD ST.
CATTE ST.
Sheldonian Theatre
Clarendon Bldg.
Bodleian Library
Hertford Coll.
Indian Institute
Radcliffe Camera
St Mary the Virgin
University Ch. of St Mary the Virgin
University College
MAGPIE LANE
Oriel Coll.
Corpus Christi College
Cathedral
ST HELEN'S PASSAGE
SQUARE
RADCLIFFE SQUARE
Exeter College
Brasenose College
Lincoln College
All Saints
Jesus College
TURL
MARKET ST.
SHIP ST.
The Covered Market
BEAR LA.
ST EDWD. ST.
Real Tennis Ct.
ALFRED ST.
Christ Church
War Memorial Garden
CHRIST CHURCH MEADOW
BLUE BOAR ST.

St John's College
Pusey House
GILES'
Blackfriars
Taylorian Institute
Martyrs' Memorial
St Mary Magdalen
Balliol College
St Michael
Playhouse
New Theatre
Oxford Union Soc.
Friars' Entry
Randolph
ST MICHAEL'S ST.
NEW INN HALL ST.
CORNMARKET
QUEEN ST.
CARFAX
Town Hall
Museum of Oxford
Museum of Modern Art
ST ALDATE'S
ST ALDATE'S
Pembroke Coll.
PEMBROKE ST.
BREWER ST.
ROSE PLACE
Campion Hall
Old Palace
ALBERT ST.
SPEEDWELL ST.
LUTHER ST.
FOLLY BRIDGE
BROAD ST.

Oriental Institute
Ashmolean Museum
Gloucester Green
Pusey House
PUSEY LA.
ST JOHN ST.
BEAUMONT ST.
BEAUMONT
GLOUCESTER ST.
GEORGE STREET
WORCESTER ST.
Worcester College
Ruskin College
WALTON ST.
WORCESTER PL.

Nuffield College
WORCESTER ST.
George
St Peter's College
NEW ROAD
CASTLE ST.
Castle
County Hall
Prison
OLD GREYFRIARS ST.
ROGER BACON LA.
St Ebbe's
ST EBBE'S
WESTGATE
TURNAGAIN LA.
LITTLEGATE ST.
NORFOLK ST.
THAMES STREET

Railway Station
Site of Rewley Abbey
HYTHE BRIDGE ST.
PARK END ST.
Quaking Bridge
TIDMARSH LA.
PARADISE ST.
PARADISE SQ.
BLACKFRIARS RD.
TRINITY ST.
FRIARS WHARF
River Thames or Isis
BOTLEY ROAD
OSNEY LA.
St Thomas
St Mary's Cemetery
Site of Osney Abbey
BECKET ST.
ST THOMAS ST.
OXPENS ROAD
HOLLYBUSH ROW